To Nancy
all my best
Love Jackie Wilson

Black Butterfly
The Journey - The Victory

Lorna Jackie Wilson

*I have told you these things, so that in me
(the Word) you may have peace.
In this world you will have trouble. But take heart!
I have overcome the world. [John 16:33]*

AuthorHouse™ LLC
1663 Liberty Drive
Bloomington, IN 47403
www.authorhouse.com
Phone: 1-800-839-8640

© 2014 Lorna Jackie Wilson. All rights reserved.

Cover Design & Portraits: Lorna Jackie Wilson
Royalty Free Images: www.Gettyimages.com

No part of this book may be reproduced, stored in a retrieval system, or transmitted by any means without the written permission of the author.

Published by AuthorHouse 07/01/2014

ISBN: 978-1-4969-1877-2 (sc)
ISBN: 978-1-4969-1876-5 (e)

Library of Congress Control Number: 2014910554

Any people depicted in stock imagery provided by Thinkstock are models, and such images are being used for illustrative purposes only. Certain stock imagery © Thinkstock.

This book is printed on acid-free paper.

Because of the dynamic nature of the Internet, any web addresses or links contained in this book may have changed since publication and may no longer be valid. The views expressed in this work are solely those of the author and do not necessarily reflect the views of the publisher, and the publisher hereby disclaims any responsibility for them.

Scripture references are KJV from
http://www.kingjamesbibleonline.org/

Contents

Dedication vii
Acknowledgments ix
Foreword xi
Introduction xiii

POETRY COMPILATION

A Child Misplaced 3
A Chosen Vessel of God 5
A Precious Gift..7
A Tragedy..9
A Tragedy in Connecticut 11
A Troubled Teen...15
Be Still & Watch the Salvation of God 19
Before You Enter Heaven..23
Belle Starr..25
Black Butterfly 29
Brown Brother 31
Celebration of Life 35
Celebrating the Life of a Minister for Christ 37
Eternal Life..39
Give in Honor to the Father...43
He's Captured Her Heart 45
I am Magnificent!..49
I'm Sorry 51
Joseph 53
Let us Give Thanks 55
Let Us See What's Real...57

Let Us Talk	61
Love & Instruction	63
Military Mirage	67
My God	71
Notes of Seasons Time	73
Pastor Mariea Claxton	75
Pure Hope	79
Regeneration	83
Remember Christ	85
Strong Black Woman	87
Teen Life in the Hood	89
The Art of Giving	93
The Beauty Within	97
The Disciple	99
The Faces We Wear	101
The Love of Siblings	103
The Meaningful Father	107
The Natural Order	109
The Ones We Love	111
The Power of One	113
The Voice of a Little Child	115
This Christmas	117
Torch of the Bold	119
What Do You Believe?	121
Why do you love me?	125
Tribute to Maya Angelou	127
About the Author	131
References	133

Dedication

To my mother, Carrie Wilson Jones (Belle Starr)

The name Belle Starr was given to my mother because of her strength and her commitment to provide and protect her children. The name in and of itself reflects the character of a notorious American outlaw. With that being said, when it came to protecting family, Carrie Wilson Jones would face great obstacles without fear. She was a very strong, opinionated woman and she carried herself with boldness. Even with this strength, she faced challenges and those challenges took on various forms. Yet through the challenges, her love was always present. Her dedication as a provider and her love for family and friends was evident to all that knew her and while her years on this earth were short, the legacy she left will always remain. With heartfelt sincerity, I dedicate, "Black Butterfly: The Journey - The Victory" to my mother, Carrie Wilson Jones. She inspired many of the passages in this book and I will always remember the journey. I love you mom.

To my mother, Acie Levingston Spraddling

There is another great mother that inspired my journey. Her name is Acie Levingston Spraddling. As I reflect on her passion and love for children, I am reminded of tireless hours of hard work, patience and prayer. I met Acie Levingston Spraddling through foster care. She provided and cared for me during a time when my biological mother faced challenges that required assistance. During those times, life was not easy. Yet, Acie introduced me to Father God and his precious son, Jesus Christ. Acie became my second mother and her love was genuine. She practiced Christianity and lived life by example. Her examples displayed amazing self-control, discipline, and holy living. She continues to help children understand their purpose in life as she guides them toward a life of self-love and family unity. God has blessed her with an amazing gift to help children facing issues associated with loss, trust and belonging. Therefore, I dedicate "Black Butterfly, The Journey - The Victory" to my mother, Acie Levingston Spraddling as well. Thank you, Acie Levingston Spraddling for everything. I could not have made it without you and Father God. I love you mom.

Acknowledgments

With sincere thanks, I acknowledge the late Bishop Vincent D. Claxton and his wife, Mariea Claxton. A full worship experience was found under their leadership. Profound guidance and sound word pricked my heart under their ministry. Together, their ministry touched the lives of many people. Their strong faith and love for God was duplicated in their works and in the lives of the people of Eagles Way Full Gospel Ministries. Through their ministry, a seed of praise was planted within my soul which led to a seed of worship and a hunger for God's word. Thank you Bishops Vincent & Mariea Claxton.

With sincere thanks, I acknowledge Bishop Ben Gibert and his wife, Dr. Charisse Gibert. After the passing of Bishop Vincent D. Claxton, my mother Acie Levingston Spraddling found anointed men and women of Christ at Detroit World Outreach in Redford, MI. Bishop Ben and Dr. Charisse Gibert embrace a church of all colors. Their ministry displays a level of diversity and unity like no other I have ever experienced. The full word of God is illuminated through real life experiences. Their examples touch on everyday living and walking in your purpose, in alignment with the perfect will of God. Thank you, Bishop Ben and Dr. Charisse Gibert.

With sincere thanks, I acknowledge my children, Wanavia, Celeste, Matthew and Christian. They are my motivation and commitment to accomplish my goals and dreams. It is my desire that they will accomplish more than they could ever imagine in life and allow no obstacle to impede their progress. May their journeys be victorious and their accomplishments, great! I love you!

With sincere thanks, I acknowledge Reginald Martin. Reginald is my close friend and confidant. He is also a writer. He has published a book of inspirational passages and understands the desire and gift to place pen to paper. His artistic ability to express experiences through real life stories is amazing. He is my encouragement to write, without abandonment, but with passion to tell the story; good, bad or indifferent. Thank you, Reggie. I love you!

Foreword

Lorna Jackie Wilson has been a blessing in my life. For the short period of time that I have known her, she has been such an inspiration to me in so many different ways. I, too, am an aspiring writer and reading Black Butterfly has made me see writing at a different level. When I first met Lorna, we discovered we had mutual interests in writing and from that we developed a beautiful relationship that I have come to cherish.

It is my belief that Lorna's mind and hands are anointed by God. She revealed to me how God would literally wake her up at night with a poem or a song. In those moments, she would immediately rise and put pen to paper. This is a gift that God has seen fit to let Lorna share with the world. In some shape, form or fashion, everyone has a message. Lorna's is the gift of poetry.

I would recommend that everyone reads Black Butterfly because this is truly the past, present and future of Lorna Jackie Wilson; a new up and coming author.

This is her time for grace and favor because the seeds that Lorna has sewn have touched lives and inspired so many that know her. Her writings allow us to see a glimpse of the journey that is clearly evident in this compilation of poetry. May God anoint this book and allow it to become a blessing to everyone who reads it.

Love Reggie

Introduction

The passion and desire to write began with deep loss, feelings of abandonment and despair. As a young girl at the age of four, I went into foster care. At the time, I did not understand why this was to become my life. I did not understand that my mother suffered from drug addiction. I did not understand why her four children were taken from her. All I knew was that my mother loved us with all her heart. During her battle with drug addiction, she underwent rehabilitation and sought to regain custody of her children from foster care. As a result, her children were returned to her and she remained clean for many years. Yet her journey led her to a path that took us from her yet again.

At the age of 16, my mother passed away and I returned to foster care. This is where I met Acie Levingston Spraddling, a foster mother after God's own heart. Acie took me in, embraced me and told me that God loved me. She desired that I come to know God and develop a relationship with Him. As I watched her life of holy living, a strong desire welled up within me to follow her guidance. This same desire inspired writing and singing. As I reflect on past experiences, both biological and non-biological, reflection takes a path through struggle and identity loss. Yet those reflections also reveal how God used struggle to shape strength, build character, and develop family stability. May this compilation of poetry inspire those with similar struggles or challenges, and may the journey illustrate the life on an overcomer.

POETRY COMPILATION

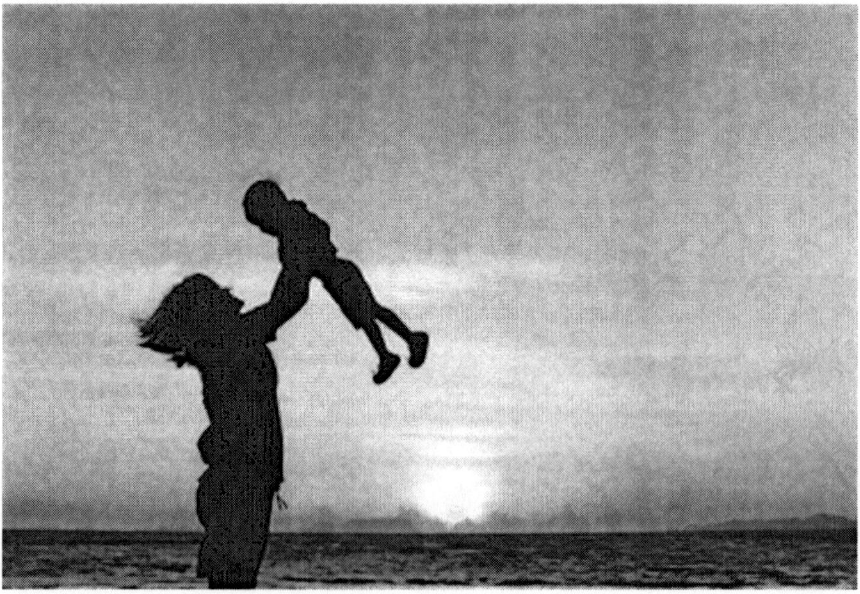

A Child Misplaced

A little one, the bond so deep, so unaware of pain conceived.
Conception that was unprepared, yet mother
clings to what they shared.
She hopes for love, does it appear? Is this a bond formed within fear?
If she connects with her small one, does she accept or does she run?

Is her decision based on love? Is her head in clouds above?
He never loved her, yet she prayed that one day he would look her way.
She thought a child would keep him close, but
it doth wrought a threat imposed.
A purpose to keep order wrapped, yet order lost itself in trap.

To disconnect, to leave in haste, the end result, a child misplaced.
Reject the love that he once knew, break or stay for he must choose.
Is he free or is he bound? Decision lacks a truth, unsound.
Responsibility grows dim. He turned his back, a sigh, a whim.

He listens to a hungry thirst, an agony found at its worst.
A child is weeping for direction, a search for warmth, a true affection.
The mother walks a lonely road, as she carries this heavy load.
Yet strength becomes a steady pace, as
one becomes a child misplaced.

To comprehend the mind of one, that is so innocent, so young,
Adoring eyes rest on her face, am I a child you find misplaced?
The folly that my mother chose, to keep you in her life so close.
A product of her own unrest, there is no plot to her distress.

This is a tale where age grows old, where there's no story to unfold.
Eyes wide open, helpless face? Why must I be a child misplaced?
Do they understand their deed? Did they fulfill a selfish need?

A struggle, I must find my way? Where does that leave me on this day?

Quite often cycle's plant a seed, a pattern prone to aid defeat.
This plight finds some in mystery, an endless fight in history.
A child misplaced can rise above to find oneself cherished in love.
Life can find a true appeal, to cure the ail that keeps one ill.

My focus must include myself, for there is beauty, there is wealth.
My family, they still have their woes.
Perchance, may I have love up close?
Treasure for all eternity, to give my life identity.
A bond with parents that waxed cold, a child
misplaced, a thread un-sewn.

To darn the stitch that forms the tie, reach
for the One that reigns "On High."
My Father's here. His bond's the mend,
embraced by hope that's found in Him.

A Chosen Vessel of God

Dedicated to Bishop Mariea Claxton

Because of the light within you, you do what
is good, what is right and true.
Because of the hope within you, each impartation flames anew.
A Chosen Vessel of God inspiring all that you beseech,
as the Word of God doth bless each and every one you teach.

Because of the joy within you, your countenance shines ever so bright.
Because of the peace within you, there is a calm, as still as night.
A Chosen vessel of God under the direction of His hand,
as the Lord of Hosts doth fill you with His purpose and His plan.

Because of the love within you, your loving kindness fills the place,
Because of your faithfulness, goodness and mercy set your pace.
A Chosen Vessel of God, so graceful, humble and meek,
as gentle as the woman that used her hair to wash Christ's feet.

Because of the strength within you, your quietness, doth yet resound.
Because Holy Spirit's within you, your living testament is profound.
A Chosen Vessel of God, a commissioned soldier for God's camp.
Anointed to pull down strongholds, with His oil to trim your lamp.

Because of the light within you, you do what
is good, what's right and true.
Because of the peace that passeth understanding,
you stand among the few.
A Chosen Vessel of God, Jesus Christ, is at your side.
As purposed to fulfill His plan, developing disciples far and wide.

Black Butterfly

Psalms 45:1-4

*My heart is overflowing with a beautiful thought!
I will write a lovely poem to the King,
for I am as full of words as the speediest
writer pouring out his story.
You are the fairest of all; your words are filled with grace.
God himself is blessing you forever. Arm yourself, O Mighty One,
so glorious, so majestic. And in your majesty, go on to victory,
defending truth, humility, and justice. Go
forth to awe-inspiring deeds.*

A Precious Gift

The gift of a mother is precious to thee,
Blossoms of love, a soft melody.
Always at hand to offer a word,
Expressions, the sweetest I've ever heard
Direction's at hand whenever it's needed,
trimmed with compassion, cultured and seasoned.
A sister, a friend and a comforter too,
with knowledge and wisdom; sound points of view.
Your life is a blessing to all that you touch
Your value is priceless and reverenced as such.
A jewel so precious, A radiance so bright,
a treasure to cherish and a joyful delight.

In appreciation for all that you do.
Thank you Mom
I love you.

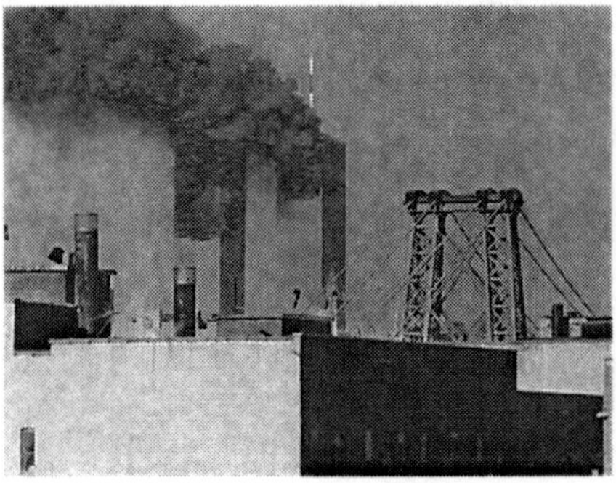

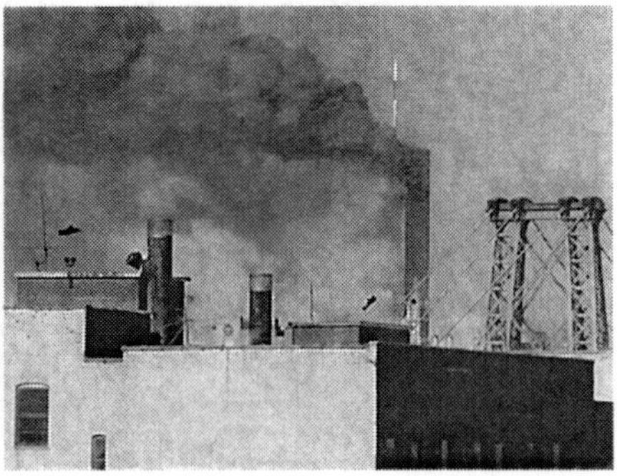

A Tragedy

Is this a dream? It can't be true. A tragic scene's come into view.
Terror unfolds before my eyes, my breath intakes, to hear their cries.

A sense of comfort, fully shaken as boeing jets sear through the nation.
It brings to mind the Harbor, "Pearl," as
well this day impacts the world.

The peace we know is surely broken. Lives
are lost and words unspoken.
An eerie crack of crumbling walls, a senseless act, unjust in cause.

The search for loved ones, name by name,
pursuit for justice we proclaim.
Is hope in tune? Our heart's true song, for liberty stands tall and strong.

A precious sight, a gift to hold as love unites to heal the souls.
We bow our heads in total silence. We pray
for peace amidst the violence.

A devastating tragedy to lose so much in history.
A havoc that can't be undone on this sad day of "9-1-1."

A Tragedy in Connecticut

Laughter and joy light up the day
As teachers teach and children play.
Then suddenly a piercing shrill.
as shots ring out and all is still.

The precious gift of human life,
found one detached from wrong and right.
A sunless day where clouds stand tall.
Where footsteps fade, a tear drop falls.

The purity of innocence.
Their love reveals benevolence.
We strive to search within the dark.
Yet search cannot reveal this heart.

Where can we go to find a light?
How can we understand this plight?
So senseless, yet we must stand strong.
To heal, for we must carry on.

For loved ones, siblings and our friends.
We must unite for we must mend.
Let's stand for what this meant to us.
Let's pray for peace, in God we trust.

Let us light a candle now,
upholding every precious child.
Each family and the teachers too.
Join hands. Unite in common view.

Let's not forget this tragic day.
It was upset in every way.
We bond, for you are not alone.
Let healing find the bright way home.

*Dedicated to the survivors of
Sandy Hook Elementary School in
Newtown Connecticut*

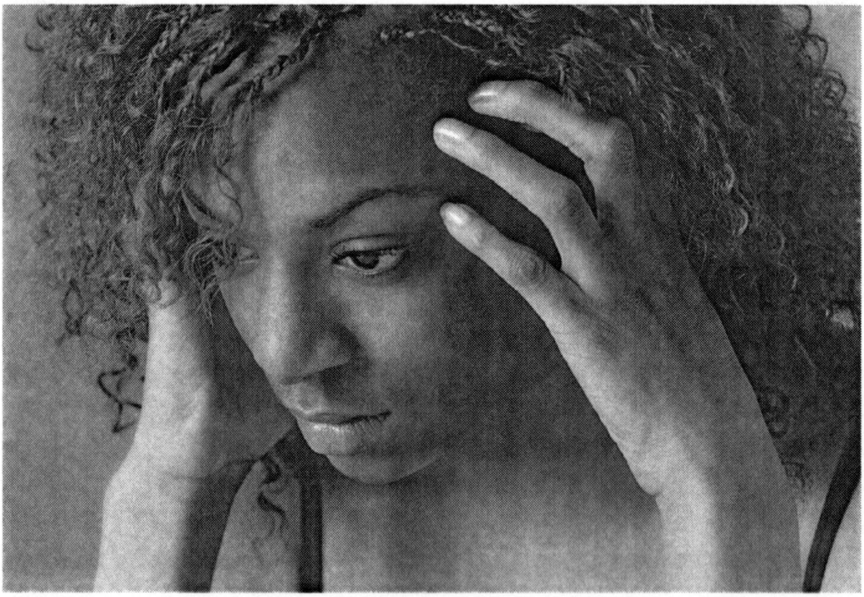

A Troubled Teen

In a world off track from thoughts of mine. In a dream, turned back, are the hands of time. In a place where I look to and fro for someone to take me from this low. Dread expressed through words unclear, maturity found in the rear.

A search for self, potential, good? A voice of wealth, misunderstood. Images, utmost despair, surface just to tear me down. Illusions ... not even prayer, touch my lips, erase my frown.

A mother, does she understand? A father, what is in his plan? My guidance, do they set the tone? All have left. I'm all alone. To contemplate self destruction, I do not fit this world's construction.
What must I do to change my views?
What leads me to the life I choose?

Dysfunction is a family trait. So why is this something I hate? Do I choose to rise above, in hope to find something I love? Will I be accepted then or will my voice fade in the wind?

A problem that I must not share, although I want someone to care. Concern's a shadow. Will I heal? My thoughts, a matter, unrevealed. Why must I feel like I belong? Does family stand proud and strong? A parentage that lacks in splendor, where growth of social skills are hindered. Do peers bond with elite in homage? Do they find traits they have in common?

Amidst the crowd, among the few,
where do I find myself, anew?
Puberty has scars that hide, beneath the surface, they
are wide. Does education have a place? Is my life a
total waste? Will my plight become assuaged? The
answers, they're not on the page.

I wander lost in my distress. What does it cost to pass the test?
Feign contentment. Leave not a clue. A guise to keep
my thoughts from view. Shut out world to build a
wall. My folks astounded when I fall.

To focus on the problem's core, do I seek help from the Lord?
When pain's too deep for thoughts to center,
I find a guide, a friend, a mentor.
A child-like faith is on the brim
of confidence found strong in Him.

Intellect grows with nutrition
developed till it meets fruition.
This is the hope that keeps me still.
It helps me cope and keep it real.

*Dedication: To any teen that has ever
struggled with identity or self-esteem.*

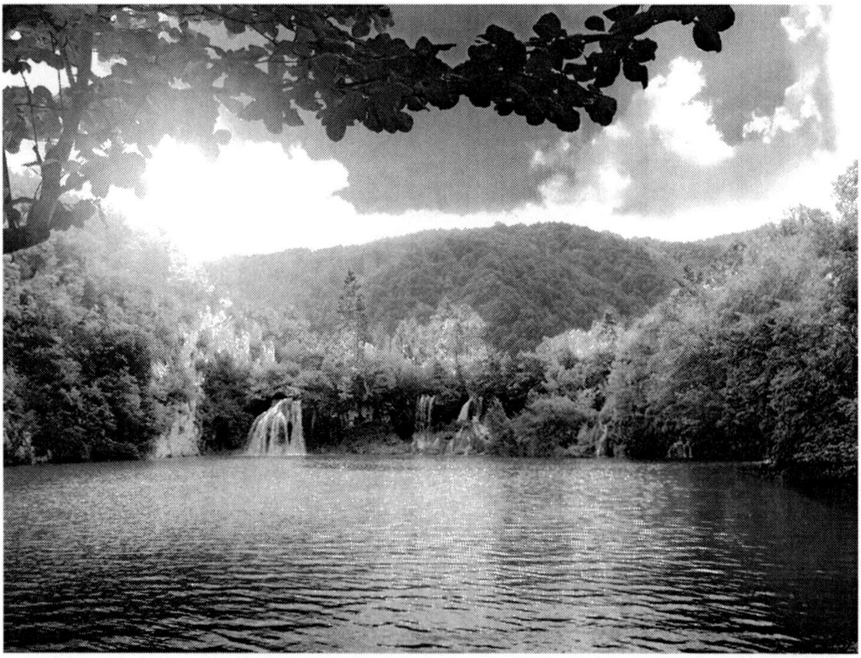

Be Still & Watch the Salvation of God

As we wander in life in search of success, some
find themselves in utter distress.
Though the journey seems long and the goal far away, hold on and be
strong, behold His great faith. Be still and watch the salvation of God.

As we labor and toil to gain fruit from the land, have we planted
a seed in another man's hand? Do we know that our blessings
spring forth as we give, as God gave His son so that we may live?

As the Israelites wandered and questioned His might,
God blessed them regardless of their blinded sight.
Miracles went forth time and time again,
yet contentment was brief, t'was the moment at hand.
Be still and watch the salvation of God.

When the heart is heavy, does one's focus lose sight? When needs
have been met, does praise reach new heights? His grace is sufficient
to carry us through; His hope, a provision for all that is true. We
need not search to and fro to find peace. His presence is nigh to
give the heart ease. Be still and watch the salvation of God.

How does one fill the void in their life? How does one offer true
sacrifice? His love's planted deep, nourished to unfurl, it never lies
sleep for it's light to the world. Circumstances come to strengthen
your faith, to promote humility, and invoke one to pray.

God knows your need before you can ask. He knows your hope, your future, your past. When do we offer God what he is due? When will we see Him outside carnal view?

He desires to fulfill your heart's most desire. Repent and prepare for consuming a fire. In whatever capacity, He prepares for your lead. Allow Him to use you wherever there's need. Enrichment of life through faith we sustain, fulfilling His purpose as we worship His Name. Be still and watch the Salvation of God!

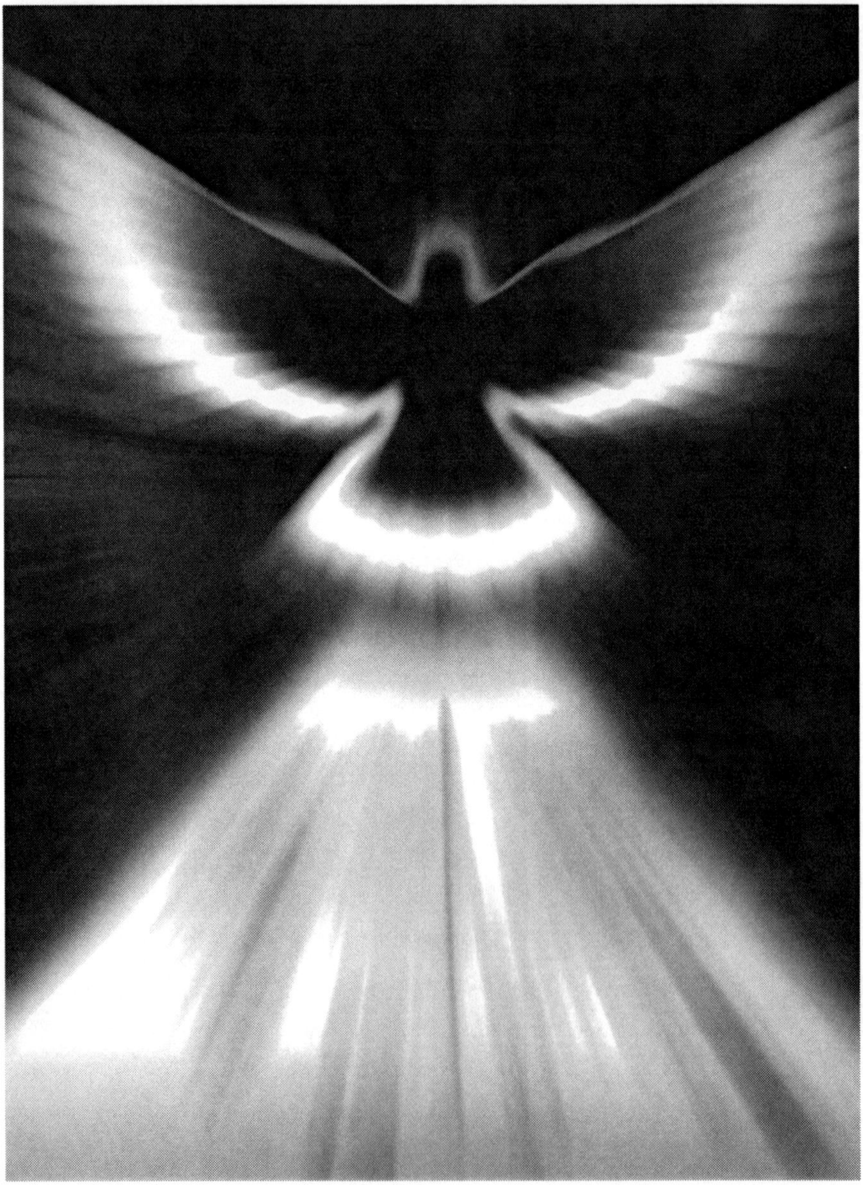

Before You Enter Heaven

Before you enter Heaven, you must acknowledge Christ.
Repent and sin no more. Forgive and walk upright.

Before you enter heaven, you must be open-handed,
Go through trials and tribulations and be able to stand it.

Before you enter Heaven, you must be meek,
Always be obedient and pray for those who seek.

Before you enter Heaven, you must be humble,
Never must you boast, brag, or grumble,

Before you enter Heaven, you must be pure in heart,
Live your life for Christ, for we are set apart.

Before you enter Heaven, you must be Holy,
Love every person and submit to Jesus totally.

Before you enter Heaven ...

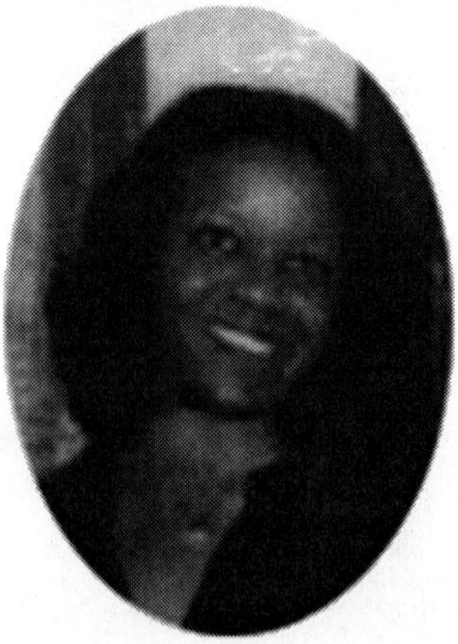

Belle Starr

- Safe in His Arms -

Belle Starr, so radiant and proud.
Mysterious woman with brilliance of style.
A woman of substance in an era of old.
A vision, a longing, a story untold.

Belle Starr, always taking a stand,
a courage so strong, a boldness so grand.
A woman of passion, a woman of taste.
A magnificent fashion of beauty and grace.

Belle Starr, mother, daughter and friend.
Connoisseur of what she desired to win.
A sister, a lover, a woman of zeal.
Misled by a plight, restored by His will.

Belle Starr, always taking a risk.
Often teetering close to the edge of a cliff.
A woman of fight, a woman of strength.
Yet gentle and sweet when it was her intent.

Belle Starr, forever protecting her blood.
Guardian mother to those whom she loved.
A provider, yet rider, to protect her children.
A fighter, survivor embracing her kin.

Belle Starr, Carrie Jones, called to go home.
May your love live strong, forever in time.
For now, know I love you, forever adore you.
A woman of spirit; yes, one of a kind.

Belle Starr, shine bright, for your life left its mark.
Your bright glowing star yet remains in my heart.
Rest now, my dear mother, no more need to fight.
For you're safe in His arms with precious new life.

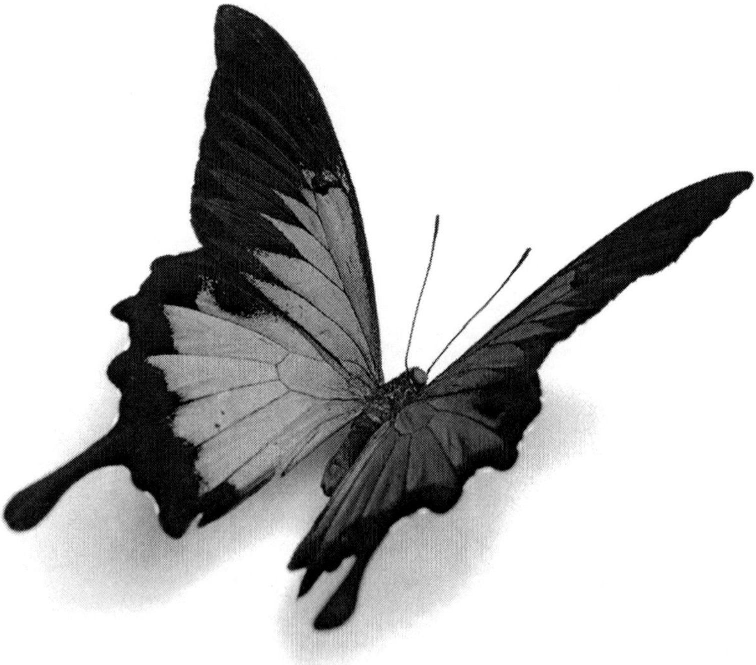

Black Butterfly

The gray steps of a wood frame home, the peeling paint and broken stone.
The ceiling stained with water spots, the sound
that makes the drip, the drop.
The eyes that roam through every room, the
lights are dim to hide the gloom.
Arise to search throughout the fray, for strength sought for another day.

The heaviness of mother's breath; she does not wake from slumbers depth.
The cares of daily circumstance confound the path of sound guidance.
The choice that takes a turn for south; the thought to take a different route.
Arise to hear the fuss, the fight, run for the door with all my might.

The streets are littered with despair. Look around, there's no one there.
The outlook speaks utter defeat; a safe haven is all I seek.
The stranger offers up his hand; he says he has a better plan.

Arise to find the claim is false, the trickery, I'm truly lost.
The friend that offers to assist; to aid the heart where there is rift.
The stumbling block at every turn, answers found through lessons learned.
The mother's cry for where she's failed. Her eyes cloud up behind the veil.
Arise to find the courtroom door. The gray steps of my home, no more.

The system, run by foster care. A stranger's arms; this isn't fair.
The introduction to new life. Hope found through the living Christ.
The tattered wings, black butterfly. The pain of loss, I often hide.
Arise, to find the pain is gone. Black Butterfly, for you are strong.

The wings that once were pale and weak. The colors are no longer bleak.
The layers mending one by one. Black Butterfly, into the sun.
The empty heart, no longer bare. Black Butterfly, into the air.
Arise, to find your destiny. Black Butterfly, and spread your wings.

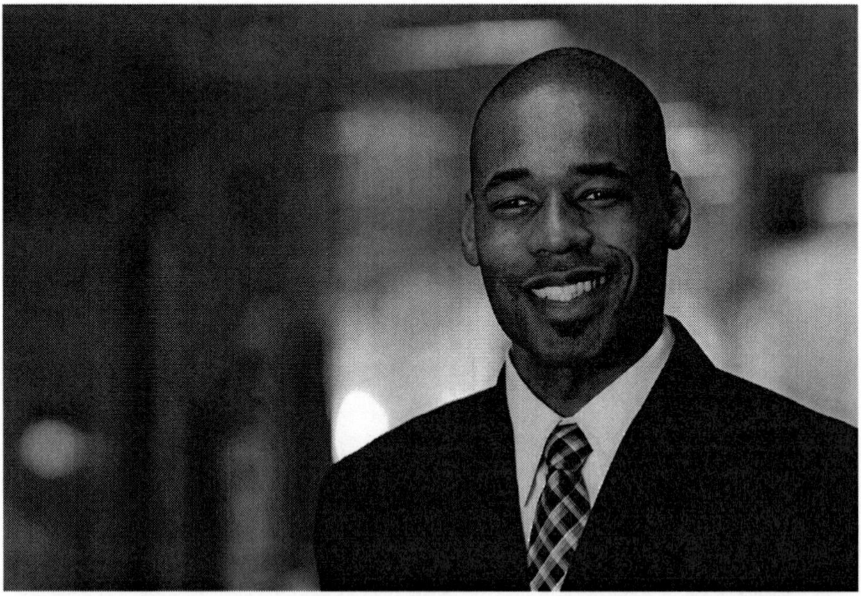

Brown Brother

Brown brother, what facet is owned?
What constitutes purpose for being?
Brown brother, have you set the tone?
What gives your life a sense of meaning?

For some say that you know them not,
and those who know you understand.
Yet no one can predict the plot,
those set for you hath yet pre-planned.

Brown brother what does set your mood?
How can one see into your mind?
Brown brother, are you understood?
What mystery is there to find?

Is there some destiny untold?
Is there a truth we must unfold?
An endless strength within yourself;
a plethora of unfound wealth?

Your strength, always so strong and true.
Your love, forever something new.
Your life, so proud, it must be told.
A gentle touch that we must know.

Brown brother, if your intellect
falls behind your friends and foes,
find courage and articulate
the depth for what we do not know.

Don't ever let someone tell you
your path leads to a sudden plight.
For you alone doth set the path,
for all you know that's true and right.

Your gift to your community will never
become lost in sight.
Face your fear, if it exists;
Stand up tall and walk with pride.

Brown brother, you will never fail;
Education is your tool of choice.
Your morale fiber is your wealth,
your intellect, your strength, your voice.

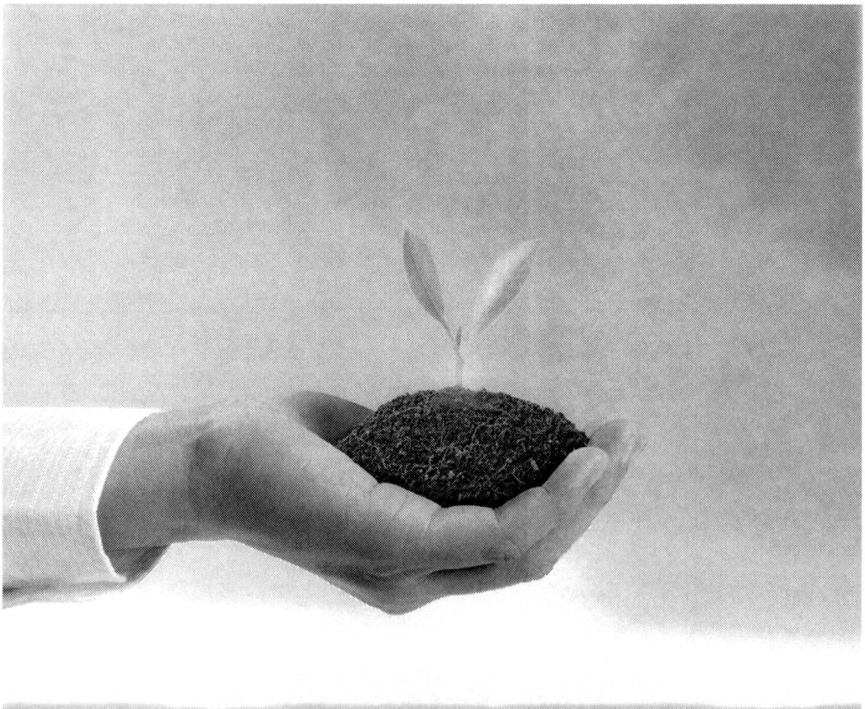

Celebration of Life

Imagine from which life was formed. The
breath of life and man was born.
The earth gave way; the ground took shift.
To honor such an awesome gift.
Dominion over land and sea. To rule with God's authority.
Do we really know the strength, by which we move through His intent?

Imagine your true destiny. To live with peace and harmony.
A life to touch; a heart to share. To give with love, to truly care.
Compassion from a precious place. To walk by faith and live by grace.
Do we really see the treasure, by which each life is truly measured?

Imagine your humanity. To seek out your serenity.
Kindness towards your fellow man. Charity, an outstretched hand.
Tolerance, is it understood? Consider what is right and good.
Do we really search to find the proper way to treat mankind?

Imagine hospitality. Effect thoughtful reality.
Considering others before self. Reward returns a new found wealth.
Benevolence, select connections. Spotlight on a self-inspection.
Reflect on why you're really here. Regard the life that is so dear.

Celebrating the Life of a Minister for Christ

- Hazel Winston Lowe -

As we reflect upon the lives of those that have touched us,
   We are reminded of their light, their laughter and love.

As we reflect upon Jesus Christ and all that is precious,
   We are reminded of His divine nature and His blood.

Hazel Winston Lowe, a daughter and a friend.
A woman of God, a soldier for Christ, a warrior Heaven sent.

As we reflect upon the lives of those that have blessed us,
   We are reminded of their devotion, prayers and faith.

As we reflect upon His Word that has filled us,
   We are reminded of His glory, mercy and grace.

Hazel Winston Lowe, a psalmist with a sword,
A woman of strength and virtue, a true gift from the Lord.

As we reflect upon the lives of those that have moved us,
We are reminded of their presence, their character and poise.

As we reflect upon His anointing and all that is Holy,
   We are reminded of His revelations and His Voice.

Hazel Winston Lowe, her joy was widely known,
A woman of passion and kindness, arise in your new home!

We love you Hazel. May you sing with the Angels!

Eternal Life

Verse:
God's love is the purest of devotion
It's the peace within my soul.
When it's found through God above—ove
Let us only seek his love.

God's love, the true meaning of the word
It can be a shield for you.
It can be a ... comforter too.
But to Him you must be true.

Chorus:
Eternal Life, it is our right, ite, ite. When you live right,
you can be free. So truly free, eternally.

Eternal Life, it is our right. He gave His Life
So let us rise. We're by His side, eternally.

Eternal Life, it is our right. For we are free,
to walk with thee, eternally. Eternal Life.

Verse:
God's love is the purest of devotion
It's the peace within my soul.
As His glory lights the sunrise,
It's the glory of His rise.

Be true to the one who's given life.
You are precious ... in His sight.
We through Him can have eternal life.
We through Him can have life.

Black Butterfly

Chorus:
Eternal Life, it is our right, ite, ite. When you live right,
you can be free. So truly free, eternally.

Eternal Life, it is our right. He gave His Life
So let us rise. We're by His side, eternally.

Eternal Life, it is our right. For we are free,
to walk with thee, eternally. Eternal Life.

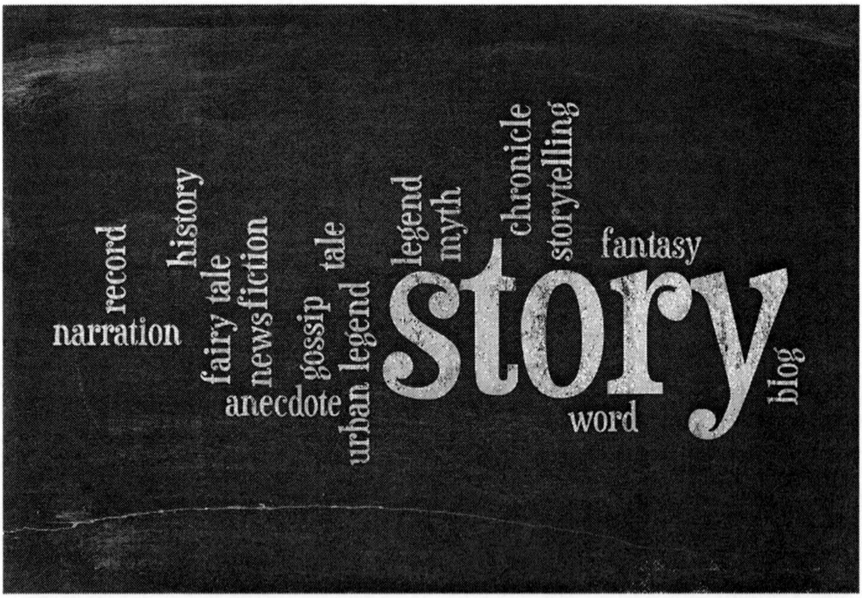
record
narration
history
fairy tale
newsfiction
anecdote
gossip
tale
urban legend
legend
myth
chronicle
storytelling
fantasy
story
word
blog

Give in Honor to the Father

I stand on behalf of Black History.
to represent the Father. He has been so sweet.

The Father has spared us to see another day,
The Father has taught us to work and to pray.

I stand on behalf of Black History.
to represent the journey through the mystery.

The Father has said we shall serve no man.
The Father has said our freedom must stand.

I stand on behalf of Black History
to represent the struggle through a misery.

The Father has brought us from a mighty long way.
The Father has given us the right to our say.

I stand on behalf of Black History
to represent the puzzle through a trickery.

The Father sheds light when all looks bleak.
The Father has given us strength to succeed.

I stand on behalf of Black History
to represent the people and the victory.

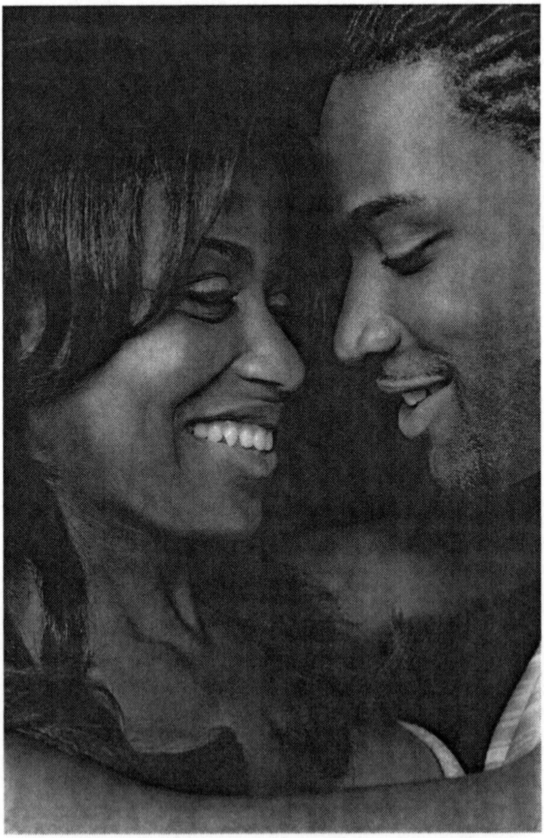

He's Captured Her Heart

A beauty walks into the room; a pair of eyes begin to loom.
He saunters towards her, preparing a spiel,
nods at the waiter, pays for her bill.
His smooth communication, a soft utterance to the ear;
while assessing her form without caution or fear.

A true gentleman from his head to his toe; polite and sincere
as he asks for her coat. Then suddenly his gaze connects
with her eyes and her heart skips a beat as he stands by her side.
The closeness of him ignites a flush in her face;
the heat of his body locks her feet in their place.

His feather-like touch is the voice that she hears,
as they move in a dance with a passion sincere.
His body in tune, their voices unheard, for she finds
herself at a loss to speak words.

The night is still young; a cool breeze strokes her lips.
He follows her rhythm and the sway of her hips.
They dance until dawn; then he follows her home.
His kiss is the gentlest she's ever known.

She reflects as she patiently waits for his call;
remembering their dance as a night at a ball.
Their intimacy, so passionate and sweet;
then comes his call by the end of the week.

Her heart is no longer her own to embrace;
remembering his touch, his lips and his taste.
He's captured her heart as no other man could.
They continue to date, 'til the date is for good.

At last, she marries the man of her dreams,
committed to love and all that it means.
He's captured her heart and their passion soars high;
their love takes new heights as content breathes a sigh.

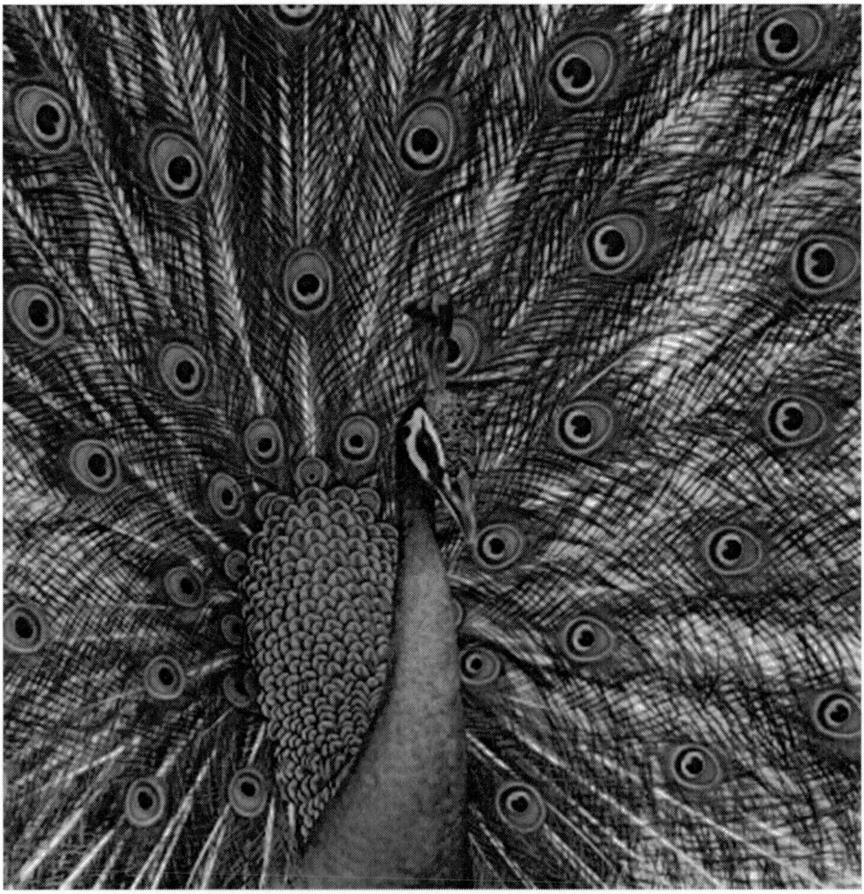

I am Magnificent!

I AM MAGNIFICENT,
GOD MADE ME THIS WAY
I AM MAGNIFICENT,
BRIGHT AS THE DAY

I AM MAGNIFICENT,
MOST PRECIOUS TO THEE
I AM MAGNIFICENT
OBSERVE AND YOU'LL SEE.

I AM MAGNIFICENT
FROM MY HEAD TO MY TOE.
I AM MAGNFICENT,
MY LIFE HAS A GLOW.

I AM MAGNIFICENT,
SPECIAL … UNIQUE.
I AM MAGNFICENT.
MAGNIFCENT ME!

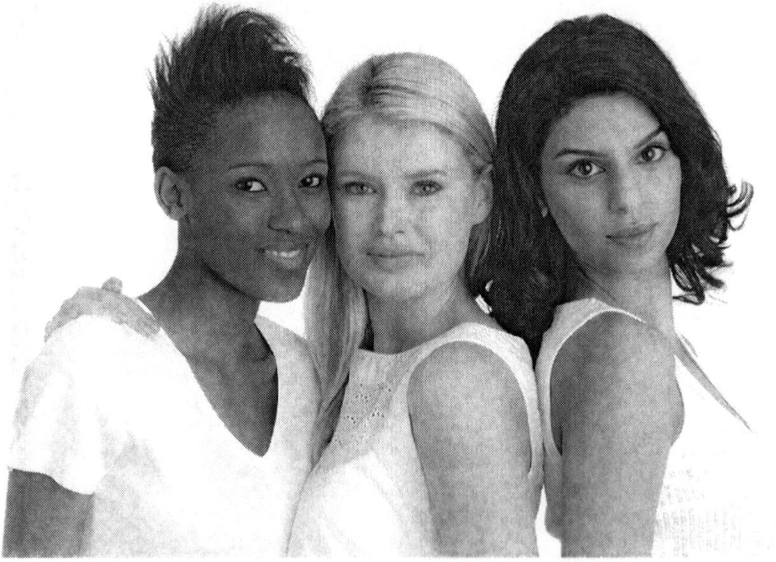

I'm Sorry

Dear friend, so kind and so sweet
Your friend is so sorry.
My heart does yet weep.
A hollow ache requires a soothe,
A friendship so precious, let us not lose.

Please accept my apology.
Mere words I not mince,
my carelessness, nor my negligence.
A friendship like ours is so precious and dear.
Our memories, imagery ever so near.

To comprehend the depth of the cost,
to cherish a heart that still weeps for a loss.
A loss of relationship, its voice yet resounds.
Let us forgive and let healing abound.

Forgive me dear friend
and let your heart mend.
Your camaraderie, a treasure;
You are truly a friend.

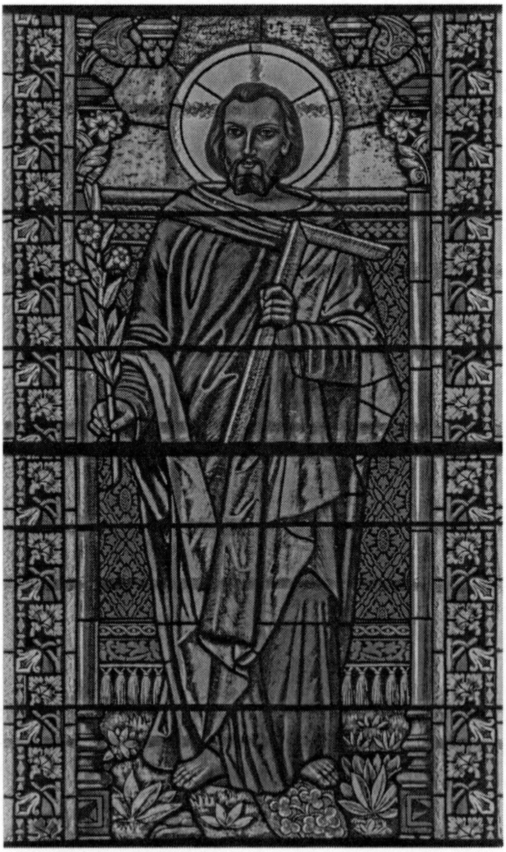

Joseph

– Highly Favored of God –

Joseph, highly favored of Israel; he was the son of Israel's old age. Given a coat of many colors for every color there is a page.

Page 1 represents his brethren and how they stripped him of his coat.
Page 2 represents the silver, for 20 pieces he was sold.
Page 3 represents his favor with a captain of the guard.
Page 4 represents his household and those under his charge.
Page 5 represents overseer; rule, an unyielding demand.
Page 6 represents dream interpretations, pharaoh, and the land.
Page 7 represents the fruit of God's blessings from above.
Page 8 represents provision through Joseph's labor and his love.
Page 9 represents the grace of God through famine, fear and doubt.
Page 10 represents a mighty hand. Through Joseph, God brought them out.
Page 11 represents goodwill towards men, and deeds ever so grand.
Page 12 represents compassion for every woman, child and man.

Now there may have been more colors than the <u>12</u> mentioned here.
Yet these <u>12</u> are the favored for the Joseph held dear.

Joseph, highly favored of God, continually worshipped His Holy name, for God's colors rested upon him. Through **HIM, God's** favor reigned.

Joseph is a fruitful bough, even a fruitful bough by a well; whose branches run over the wall. Genesis 49:22

Black Butterfly

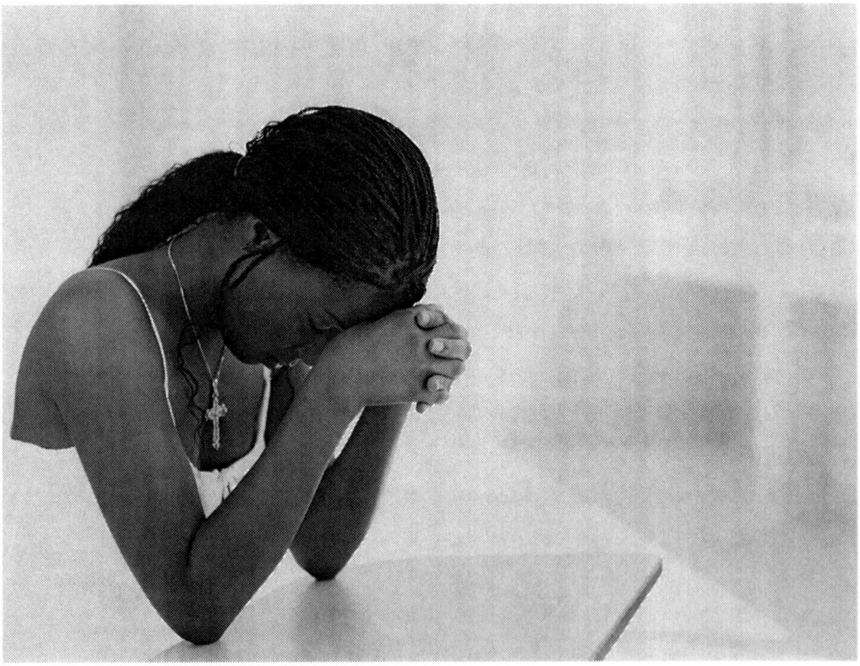

Let us Give Thanks

Dear Heavenly Father, we give thanks for this day,
With reverence, your favor reminds us to pray.
We thank you for kindness, for mercy and grace.
We thank you for family, for oneness of faith.

With ardor, we serve thee, delight in the task.
Thank you for giving us all that we have.
Extending a hand to those that have need;
reaping the gift from the fruit of its seed.

Comfort for one that seeks shelter from cold.
An offer of warmth in one's humble abode.
Sweet savors assail with aroma's sublime,
as families await for the moment to dine.

Through colonies of old, through our country's fruition;
generations unfold this family tradition.
Let us give thanks for the blessings of love,
for the mercies bestowed from the Father above.

Let us give thanks for the bountiful land,
for the harvest is ripe, tis the might of His hand.
Through times of great famine, abashment draws nigh,
through conflict and lament withstanding its plight.

Let us give thanks for the victories of war,
the freedoms of choice, the hope from the Lord.
His grace is sufficient to carry us through.
His strength's a provision, for honor and truth.

Let us give thanks for the blessings grandeur.
Let us not take for granted this great country's allure.
As we share with someone less fortunate than self,
reward's found within, tis the beauty of wealth.

Dear Lord, we give thanks.

Let Us See What's Real

(Character and Conduct)

The people we meet each and every day.
What influences are portrayed?
Does character or conduct bear a style of life?
Does teaching or rearing instill a sense of pride?

Status or social standing, where does it fit in?
Are the socially elite the only ones that win?
Does education or relationship bear on path of choice?
Does economic status exude the proper poise?

The language we speak and the dialect of use,
Is it articulate or purposely dilute?
Does selection of a friend depend on certain cliques?
Does integrity have meaning? What make a friend legit.?

A genuine sincerity, a purity of heart,
A character of truth that should not ever part.
It starts from the day we first meet eye to eye.
It starts from the moment we learn what's wrong from right.

The people we meet each and every day.
The window of their soul is in every word they say.
Body language is important and it is also key.
It provides the subtle hints, in action and in deed.

Black Butterfly

Eye contact as well renders all else moot.
Diverted towards the floor. Do they speak the truth?
Character and Conduct. It takes on many forms.
Often words unspoken yet on the sleeve are worn.

Observe and you will find the hidden through the clues.
Assess so you can see a clearer point of view.
Character and Conduct. Let it be revealed.
Removing all pretense. Let us see what's real.

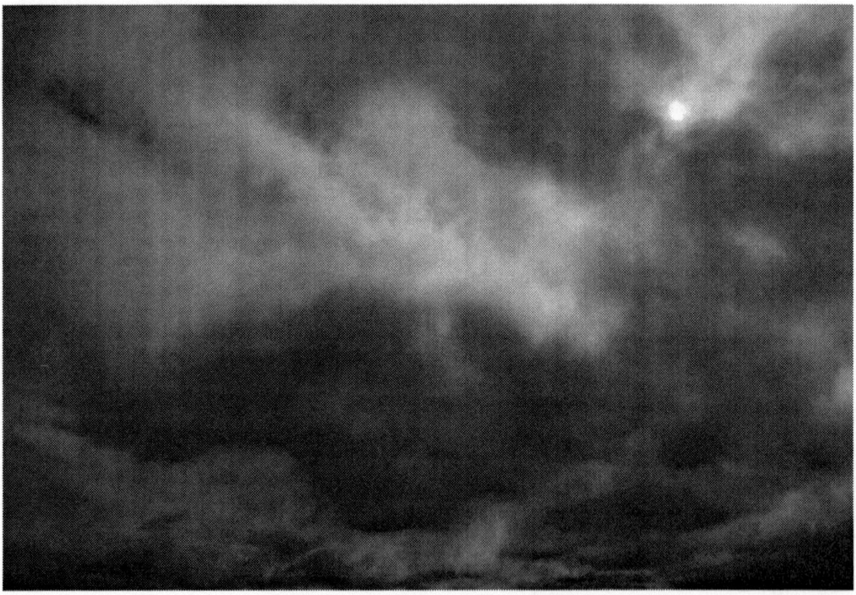

Let Us Talk

The inner thoughts that we don't share,
to guard our hearts from life's despair.
The fragile string, the thread, so fine.
The whispering, words lost in time.

Your fear is real, rejection's nigh,
yet there is chance and it soars high.
Do we take solace in words unspoken,
in hope to keep our lives unbroken?

The voice of reason, a silent prayer,
when we feel no one really cares.
Misunderstanding has no place.
Come let us talk, face-to-face.

A will to listen, a voice for thought,
with ears of patience, no search for fault.
Love and kindness set the pace.
The past behind us, the pride abased.

Dispelling anger, we reach the goal,
for peace and oneness does unfold.
Let us talk and bond together,
we'll calm the tides of stormy weather.

Love & Instruction

As we endeavor to instruct the ones that we love,
do we provide examples in the lifestyles we lead?
As we endeavor to correct the ones that we love,
do we encourage them in what they believe?

As we endeavor to advise the ones that we love,
do we take time to listen to youth?
As we endeavor to chastise the ones that we love,
are our ears inclined to hear what is true?

As we endeavor to embrace our children in love,
do we incorporate laughter and fun?
As we get caught up with cares of our lives,
are moments captured more likened to none?

When children are rebellious and truth hard to find,
do we seek counseling to condition the mind?
As we consider kindness, anger or wrath,
Are decisions aligned on the right path?

As we endeavor to embrace our companion,
do we cherish vows of love from conception?
As we endeavor to trust our companion,
do we cloud truth with deceit and deception?

As we endeavor to lead in the home,
do we feel a compelling desire to flex
or does the weight of our foot bear so heavy a load,
Till the burden or weary takes form as perplexed?

As we endeavor to guide in the home,
Are we secure in our stance as the lead?
Do we afford others the right to freedom
to pursue their own goals and fulfill their own needs?

When our lives are unbalanced and confusion is nigh,
where lies our hope in this instance?
Do we separate and run to our own separate rooms
or retreat somewhere in the distance?

As we endeavor to instruct the ones that we love,
communication should always take precedence.
The voice of each and every one is significant.
May it be heard throughout every residence.

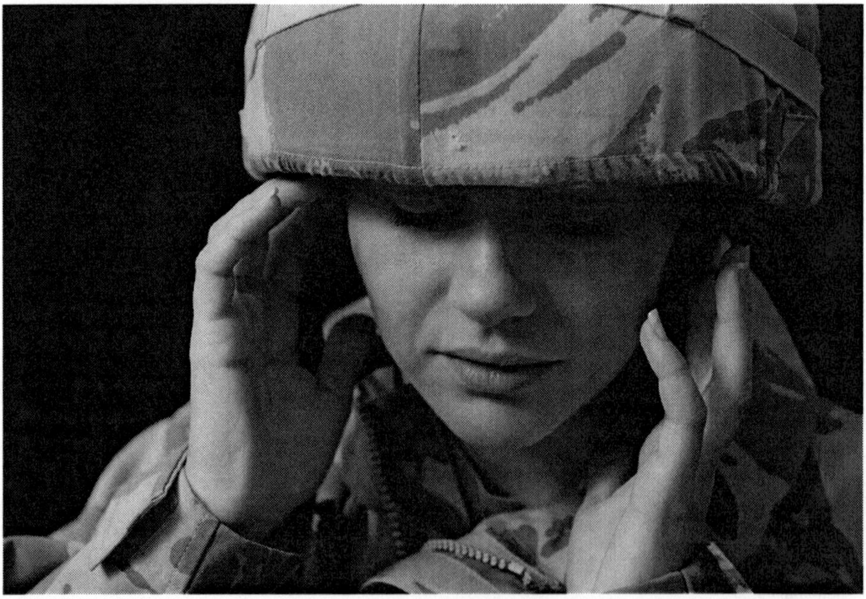

Military Mirage

As I sit, I reflect on a plan to pursue,
armed forces enlistment to protect country views.
Views that are founded on power and land,
political interests, all parts of the plan.
I read and I ponder the oaths of convention;
I sign to attain a dissimilar intention.

I arrive on the scene with my luggage in tow;
recruits are in hundredths in lines by the row.
There are drill sergeants running,
one yells in my face and I wonder what's happening.
How did I get to this place?

Were my visions and goals a mirage in my mind?
Will they ever be realized in my sense of time?
My training is vigorous and my friendships grow fast;
graduation attained at the top of my class.

With honors in skills where one seeks to achieve,
does mission transcend goals that once were perceived?
Surely, my goals seem much closer in sight.
Then I get orders; I ship out at first light.

I fight for a war; can't remember the cause.
There's death all around me. Smoldered ash in the fog.
My country's impressed. My family's all there.
Yet the mind is so stressed. I'm still out there somewhere.

My service to country in exchange for my goals?
Will I ever attain them? Somehow I must know.
The answer's inside me; I find strength to go on.
With God right beside me, I must weather this storm.

A lesson is learned as mirage fades with time.
My vision is clear as peace restores mind.
Let commitment to country be your reason to fight,
while your focus on goals remain at hindsight.

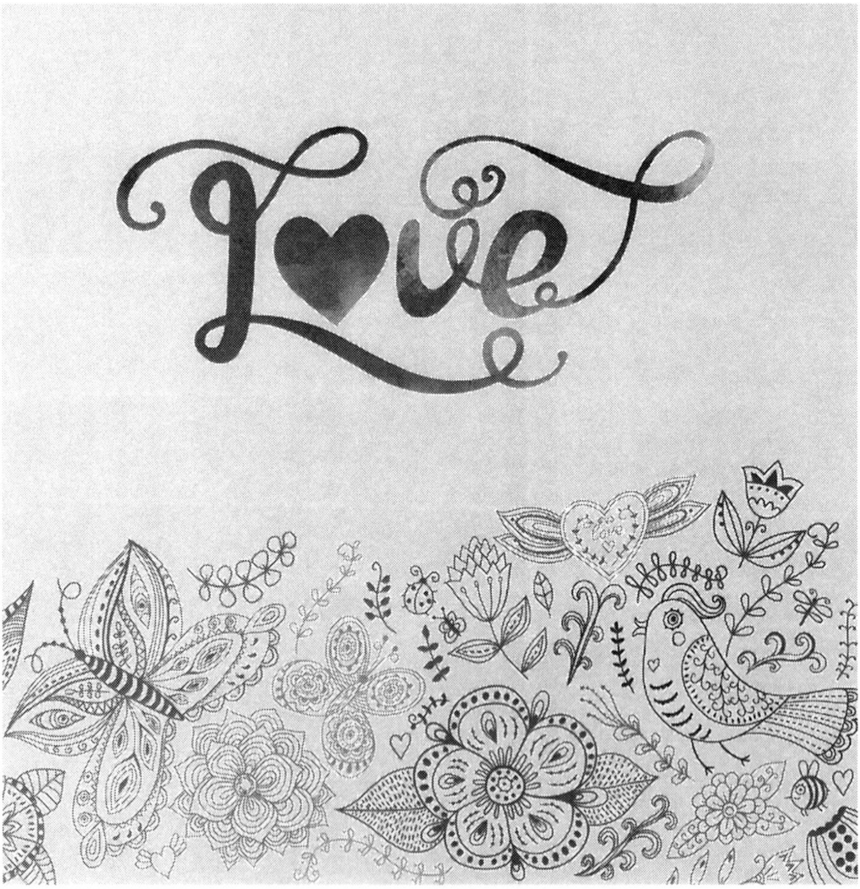
Love

My God

My God has an everlasting love for me.
He is my joy, my strength, and my victory.

My God is God and there is none other
except Jesus Christ, His son, my brother.

My God sent His son so that we might be saved
He died for our sins and He rose from the grave.

My God is a healer, His truth is the light.
My footsteps are ordered by His power and might.

My God is a mighty God of righteousness
His eyes, His hands, His feet are blessed.

My God is a savior, awesome and grand.
The author of pure love, the creator of man.

My God created Heaven, earth, even hell.
My God can do anything, anything but fail.

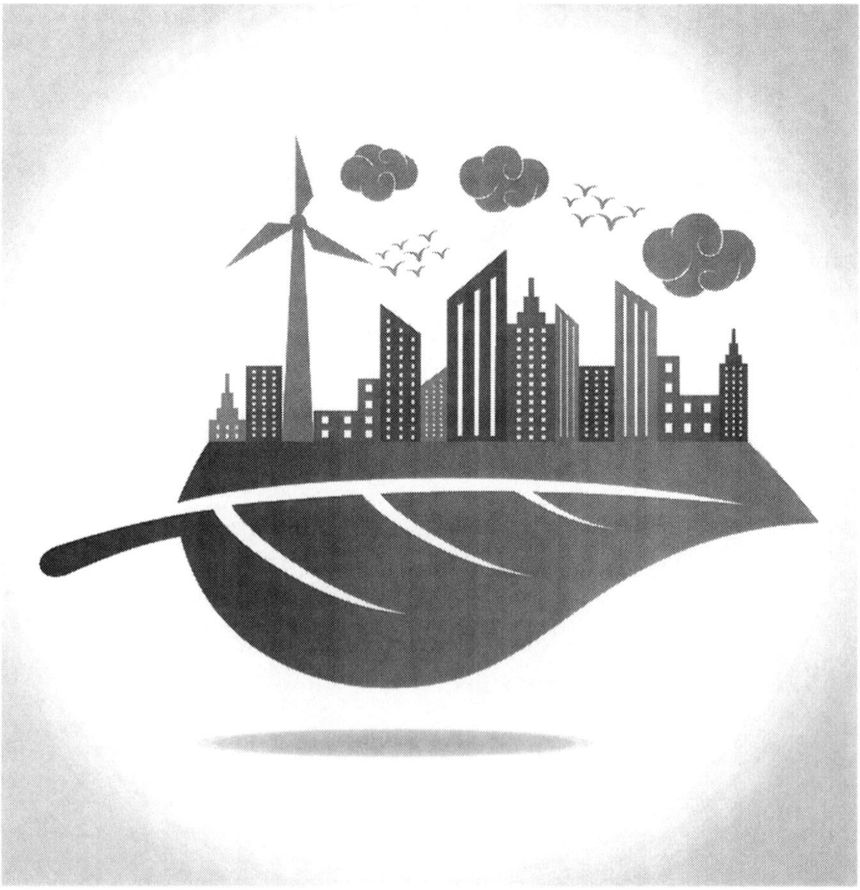

Notes of Seasons Time

On cloudy days, does one conform,
as sun sets low and shadows warmth?
Moods may change with seasons time,
like melody's found on a chime?

Can you hear within the tones,
a gentle breeze so softly blown?
The tone is light and crystal clear,
a whisper close, a peace so near.

Perfect view when skies are gray.
See the notes of golden rays.
Colors, bright; vibrant, distinct.
Define the shades, name the links.

A beauty, such, we must behold,
a radiance, found uncontrolled.
A breath of air, so pure and clean,
a freshness that one hopes to glean.

In doleful times, heart's at peace,
for tones of gaiety bring ease.
Seasons may depict the mood,
ambiance to calm and soothe.

Fragrances that one may wear,
sweet aromas in the air.
Place a smile upon my face,
someone's frown may be erased.

Flickering lights, rays of gold,
a gentle touch my heart unfolds.
What does one hear with season's time?
What melody's found on the chime?

Poise adjusts with seasons time,
and often finds a path divine.
Sorrow, joy, a world apart,
a precious light within the dark.

A pleasant song so sweet and dear?
A woeful song to shed a tear?
One must choose the note that's played.
What sets the mood for you today?

Pastor Mariea Claxton

A pastor walking in her purpose.
In the Spirit of God's pure light.
Developing a family of believers
    Being led by Jesus Christ.

Ministering to a secret place that some
    find unrevealed. Calling forth with
    clarity God's purpose and His will.

A pastor, a mother, a counselor and a friend.
A woman of great compassion, so set apart from sin.
    With loving kindness, God has drawn us
    unto His sweet embrace and given us a shepherd
        with honor and with grace.

As she seeks to hear from God, she sups with Him in prayer.
He fills her with His Word, His truth is always there.
This woman lives a Holy life with valor for the cause.
We must join her in the battlefield; prepare to win the lost.

I am thankful for her faithfulness, her tenacity and her strength.
She takes on the Great Commission with wisdom Heaven sent.
Revelation of His Word rests upon her as a dove.
Developing God's disciples, imparting knowledge through His love.

She demonstrates the attributes for living the exchanged life.
Applying biblical principles through the Power of God's might.
Can't you see the vision? Can't you see the growth?
The path is set before her by the awesome Lord of Hosts.

We are blessed to have the privilege to listen and to learn.
A ministry so unique like the bush that never burns.
This precious jewel illuminates the Glory from on High.
An anointing sent to cover us. Don't let it pass you by.

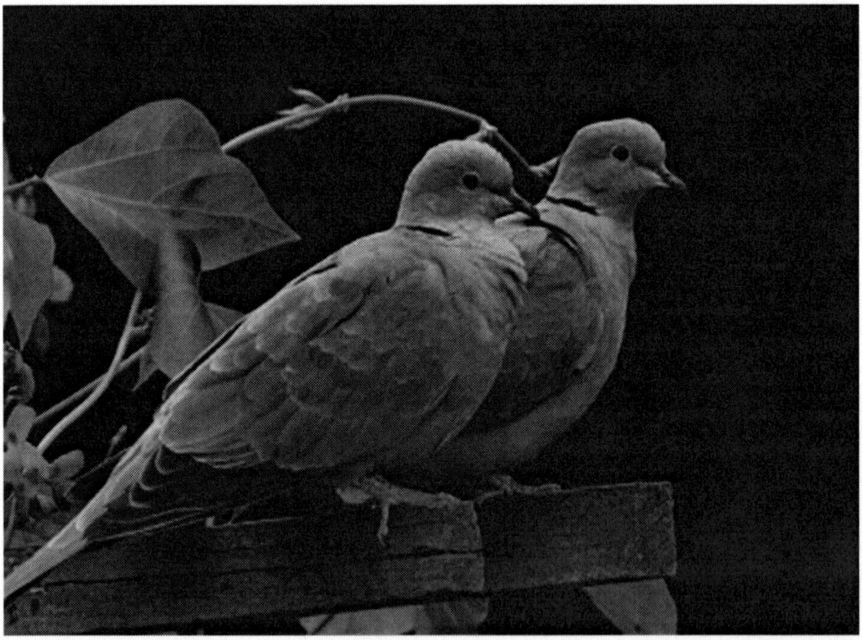

Pure Hope

– How faith is defined –

How does one define his faith? Is it tangible to touch?
Where lies the substance of the hope that one claims to be as much?
Faith is the substance of things hoped for
and the evidence of things unseen.
Yet some must see, to believe that God yet intervenes.

How does one define his faith? What miracles must one see?
Where lies the confidence, the trust? In what does one believe?
Faith performeth works, for works without faith is dead.
Where lies the work that proves ones worth, by what faith is one led?

How does one define his faith? Does one even have a clue?
Where lies the hope that leads him to the one that holds the truth?
Faith is purity of hope for pure hope cleanseth the soul.
The Word sharpens the iron with fire that forms to shape the mold.

How does one define his faith? To whom do we adore?
Where lies the call to follow His law and love forevermore?
Faith is abounding love. Does it mend the broken hearted?
Where lies the love that ministers to the weary and downtrodden?

How does one define his faith? Is it based on a belief?
Where lies the evidence; the proof, one aspires to achieve?
Faith is always continual for it never ceases to advance.
Where lies the Songs of Zion to light the joy within the dance?

How does one define his faith? Is it evident in all we do?
Jesus Christ, the cornerstone; the Hope of Glory, pure and true.
Faith is waiting for direction as waters wait, ever so still.
While walking in His purpose, flowing according to His will.

How does one define his faith? By what is treasured as we give,
by the peace of God, the love of Christ, and the Word in which we live.
Faith is purity of hope for pure hope cleanseth the soul.
It is the burning instrument of God that sears and makes us whole.

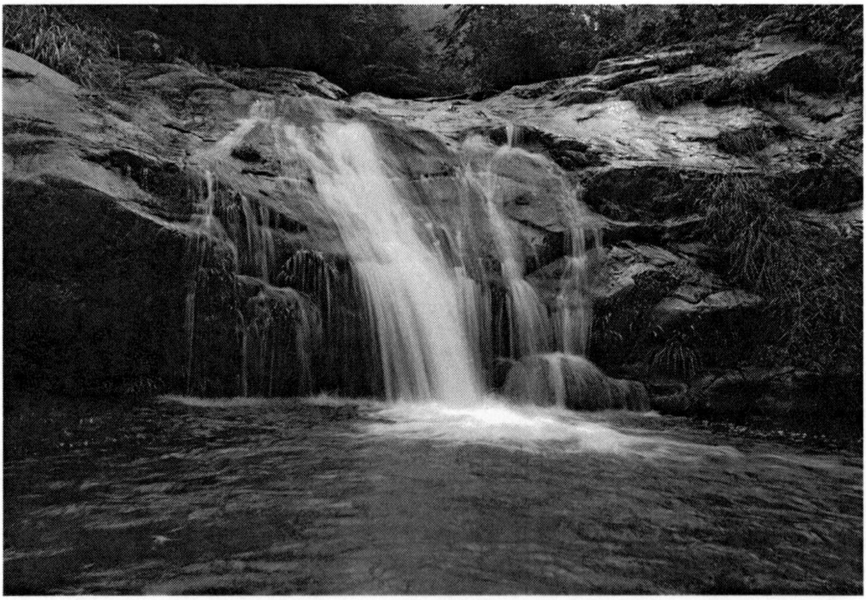

Regeneration

For every creation, there is a molding taking shape.
For every creation, all men should diligently seek His face.
For the regeneration of His people must start from within.
Transformation only begins when we separate from sin.

For every creation, salvation was bought with a sacred price.
For every creation, present your bodies a living sacrifice.
For the regeneration of His people invokes Holy Spirit from on high.
Holy Spirit comes to convict the flesh we crucify.

For every creation, through the heart rebirth takes place.
For every creation, repentance and confession set the pace.
For the regeneration of His people; we know that He yet reigns.
True praise and worship serves to honor His precious, Holy name.

For every creation, there is a hunger and a thirst.
For every creation, there is longing for rebirth.
For the regeneration of His people, His Word abides as pure light.
Rededication to God's purpose, restores hope and draws us nigh.

For every creation, let our prayers intercede for one-another.
For every creation, the love of Christ embraces every brother.
For the regeneration of His people, His name we truly bless.
Giving Him glory, honor, and praise for His awesome holiness.

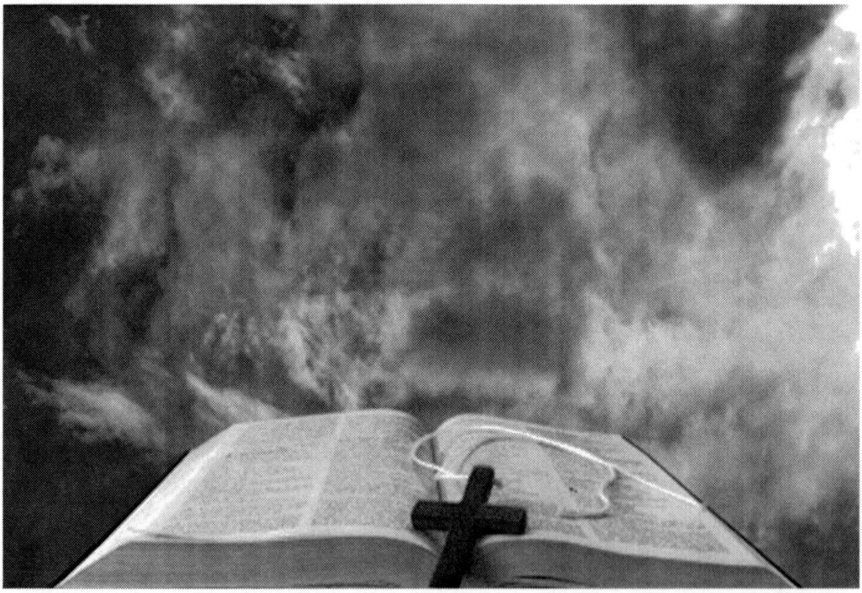

Remember Christ

Looking above at the stars so bright,
I see a sparkle in the night.
It shines and lightens up the sky.
So beautiful this light on high.

Its meaning is sharp as a two-edged sword,
Yet, it represents the coming of Christ Jesus, our Lord.
With reverence we worship, await and we pray,
following His guidance each and every day.

Whenever we need Him, He gives us His hand.
He tells us through trials, His children must stand.
He has taught us His Word so our minds won't be dazed.
So let us take time out to give Him the praise.

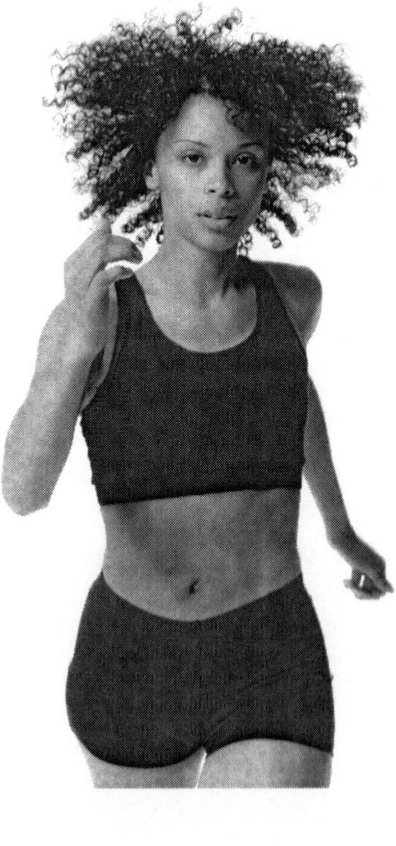

Strong Black Woman

Strong black woman, extraordinary in fortitude.
Her composition envelops experiences that define her strength.
As each challenge measures ability and tests her faith,
she finds endurance through dedication to achievement.

Strong black woman, unique in mindset.
Her courage produces positive results and elevates expectation.
As each journey supplies knowledge and understanding,
she finds enlightenment through focus on direction.

Strong black woman, affectionate in love.
Her compassion is reflected through the mirrors of her eyes.
As her family is cherished and each member rests assured,
she finds jewels of a treasure surround her in adore.

Strong black woman, exceptional in benevolence.
Her selflessness encourages those enamored by her presence.
As each life is influenced by the guidance of her touch,
she finds beauty through tenacity and inspires one's advancement.

Strong black woman, devoted in her faith.
Her daily walk with Christ is the true source of her strength.
As connection with the Father embraces relationship with Him,
she finds joy, restoration and ability to strive on.

Strong black woman, you have made a difference in this world.
Your accomplishments convey a multitude of pride.
Thank you for your commitment and your undying love.
You are the thread that knits the pattern in the fabric of our lives.

THANK YOU ... Strong Black Woman!

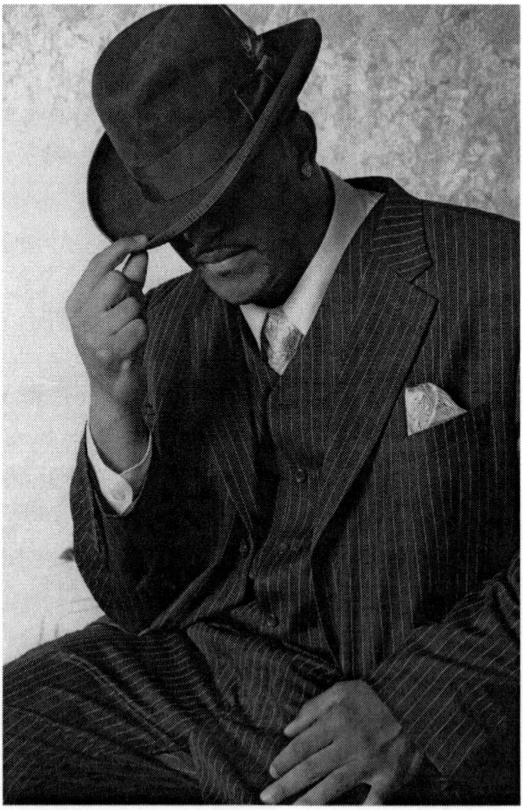

Teen Life in the Hood

The grass is tall. The weeds spread broad.
The air is filled with smoke and smog.
The streets are littered with debris.
The people shout profanity.

Then a young girl walks the road.
Surrounded by a world so cold.
A friend crosses. Her head held low.
She shares the story of a foe.

The neighbor's porch. The street girls sit.
They throw the rocks. Our legs, they hit.
The knife that's held up to her throat.
The fear within her eyes is told.

Then into the house we run.
We try to hide from wrath to come.
The girl thought that she hit a wimp.
Then at the door we face her pimp.

The pimp is hard. The voice is rough.
The threat to take a life, no bluff.
The rush to find a different home.
The need to find a different zone.

The foster home. The different house.
The new parents. A different route.
The teen that lived within the hood.
The house she left behind for good.

Then into a new found life.
The hope to find a different side.
Knowledge brings a different plan.
Yet memories will always stand.

The foster home. The knowledge gained.
The family. Our ties remain.
The love dispels all that was wrong.
The journey served to make her strong.

Dedicated to Deborah Holloway

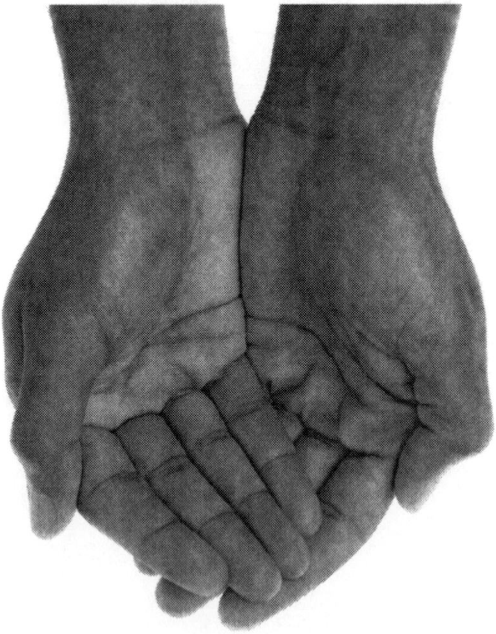

The Art of Giving

The art of giving begins with a vision,
a vision to see the abundance of life.
A vision for those that are hungry and crying;
a vision for those that are striving yet dying.

The art of giving begins with change
for nothing ever changes unless action is taken.
The action of voicing the quest far and wide.
The action of enduring opposition with pride.

The art of giving begins with a pure heart;
a heart for those less fortunate in life.
A heart for those we see every day;
affluent and indigent along the way.

The art of giving begins with change
for nothing ever changes unless action is taken.
The action of standing when one feels he can't stand.
The action of planning without resources at hand.

The art of giving begins with a calling;
a calling to speak for those yet unheard.
A calling for those seeking fairness and honesty,
among the classes of status and the masses of policy.

The art of giving begins with change
for nothing ever changes unless action is taken.
The action of affecting those united in cause.
The action of changing proposed bills into laws.

The art of giving begins with everyone;
everyone pulling together and reaching out.
Reaching out to those young and old;
reaching out to people, homeless and cold.

The art of giving begins with change
for nothing ever changes unless action is taken.
The action of pledging a commitment, a vow.
The action of compassion and love begins NOW!

... The Art of Giving

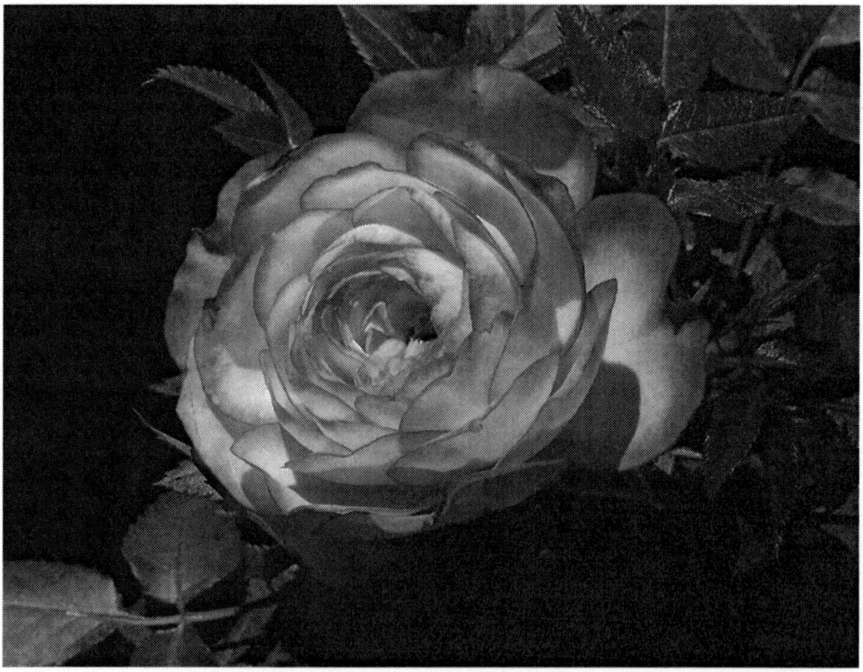

The Beauty Within

Have you ever been told beauty is in the eye of the beholder,
yet the beholder only values what the naked eye can see?
Is one's beauty merely external, softer or colder,
Or can one look beyond surface, beyond view of skin deep?

Have you ever been told that your hair is too short,
your eyes too small, your statue too large?
Yet opinion of character so commonly misplaced,
where misperception of character is often the case?

Have you ever been told that you do not fit in?
Does status or rank measure character's ascent?
Your dedication to give one hundred percent,
or is level of character defined from within?

Have you ever been told that your gift is so rare,
its beauty shines upon the countenance of face?
and the love that you share is a beacon of light;
a radiance captured by its own special grace?

So often we can't see the truth or the light;
searching the surface for external delight.
when the beholder is akin to a clouded lense;
forever longing, not conceiving that the beauty's within.

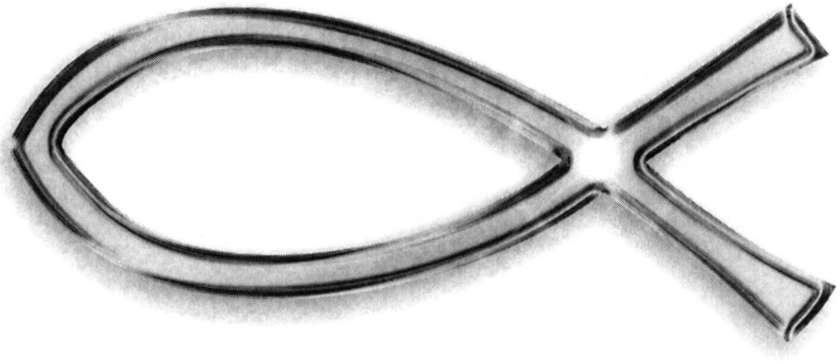

The Disciple

– As We Follow Christ –

As we follow Christ, we find guidance, His direction.
As we follow Christ, there is solace in correction.
With persistence, we strive to be like thee.
His Word, true life; the air we breathe.

As we follow Christ, we must embrace the cross.
As we follow Christ, let us gather the lost.
Expect a great harvest, thank God and rejoice.
His Will is explicable. Heed to His voice

As we follow Christ, a lamp exudes our life.
As we follow Christ, Praise Him. He's magnified.
With ardor, we minister wherever there is need.
A vessel used by God in spirit and in deed.

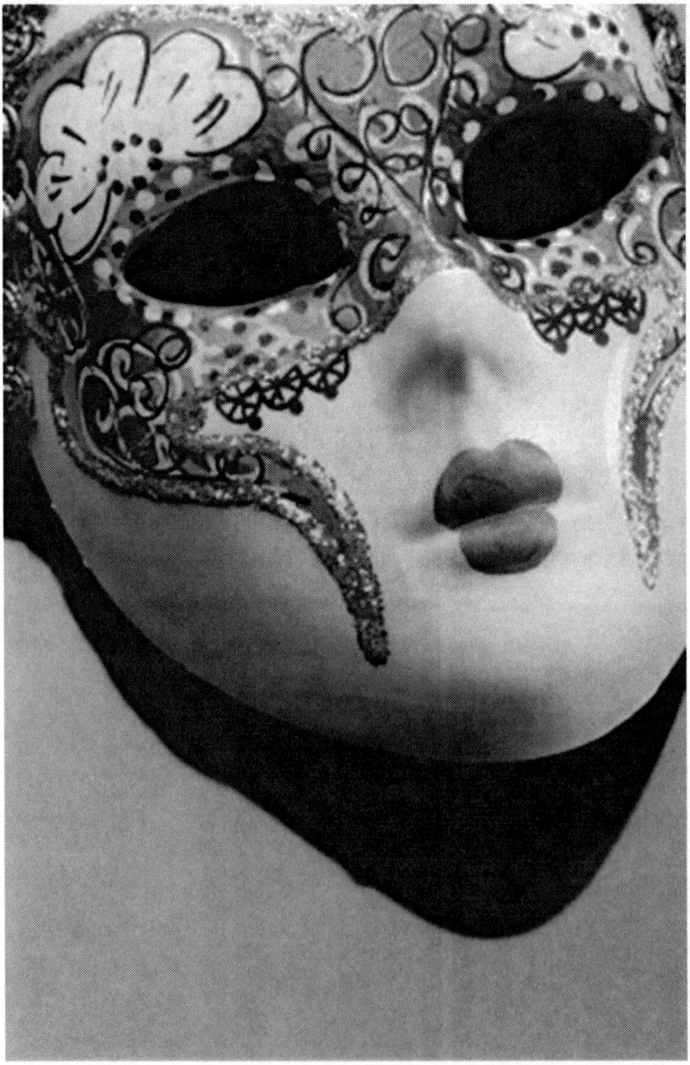

The Faces We Wear

A pretense of love to solicit a friendship.
A façade of acceptance when forming a kinship.
The faces we wear, void of honor and truth.
Deceit is its name. Shame is its proof.

The faces we wear, the falsehoods of notion.
Climbing the ladder for success and promotion.
Where is integrity? What does it matter?
Do we find remorse when lives have been shattered?

The faces we wear puffed up with vain glory.
Judgment on status when all have a story.
A message to those that find themselves wearing,
the habits of old, their faces uncaring.

The faces we wear reflect the right fruit,
peace trims the vine, pure love at its root.
The eyes are compassion, the lips do not lie.
We inhale a pure savor, so sweet from on high.

The faces we wear permit the image of Christ
to dwell in our hearts, to reign in our lives.
As the light of the Lord brightens your face,
duplicities severed for truth's in its place.

Why must we wear faces when God gave His Son,
to erase all the faces except the True One?
Hold on to the beauty, its visions of awe.
Our faces are cleansed by the power of God.

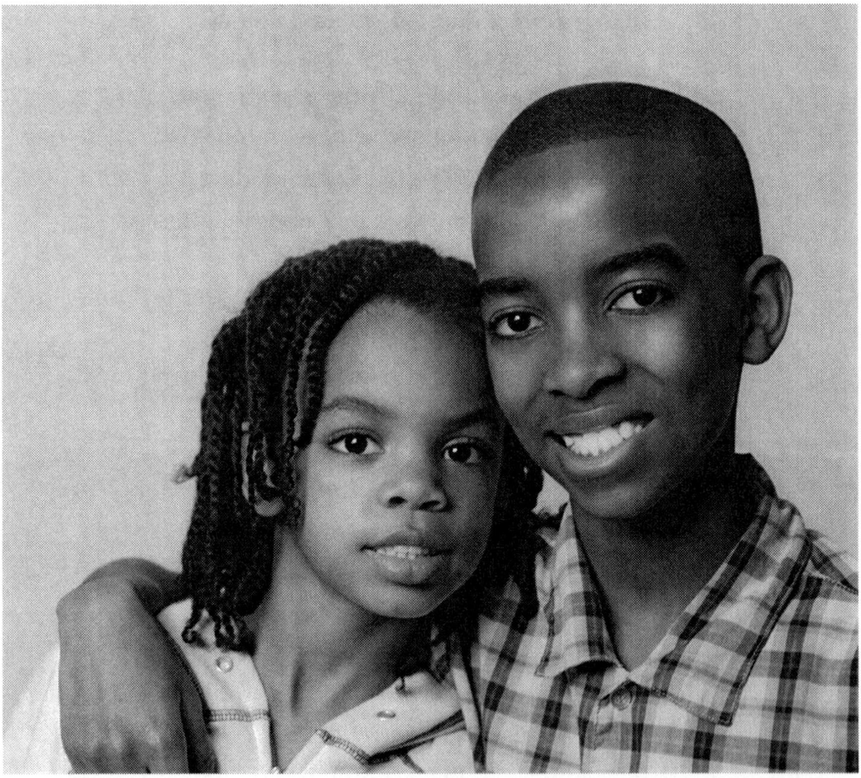

The Love of Siblings

As a little child opens her eyes to see the morning sun,
she considers her day and all that will be fun.
She looks to her siblings to decide what they shall do,
never understanding exchange in the next room.

People are talking and discussing where she will go.
This includes her siblings while her mom walks to and fro.
Then without warning, we are rushed into a car.
Tears stream down softly as we're torn and ripped apart.

The siblings are divided, and the pain is to the core.
The break so overwhelming for the siblings are no more.
Into separate homes, each sibling must reside.
Never understanding, what has happened in their lives.

Some foster homes were kind with values strong and clear.
While others unrelenting, instilling sorrow among fear.
The stories I could tell you of a journey through a storm.
The memories I recall of the hope that turned to mourn.

The years went by so fast and through time age took its toll.
Yet the siblings reconnected, restoring love into the fold.
Today each child remembers the struggle and their strength,
never forgetting their bond and all that it has meant.

The love of siblings, stronger today than yesterday.
Experiences remembered through the choices that they made.
Forever my brother, my sister, we endured our history.
Our love truly restores us as it mends the family tree.

Dedicated to my brother & sister
Robert & Arnetta Wilson

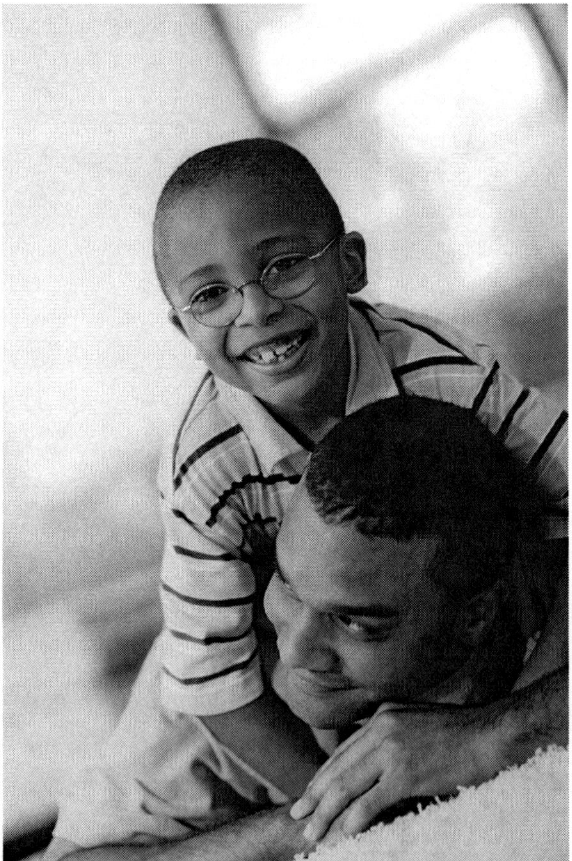

The Meaningful Father

I know a God who is proud of the man,
The man, he created from dirt and from sand.

I know a God whom needeth not bother,
to explain his creation, the meaningful father.

The father who's blessed for the love he doth bring.
The love of the mighty and powerful King.

The father who's worthy to be called by the name.
The name of the father who walks without shame.

A father that nourishes and cares for his young.
A father that loves and provides for his son.

A father that cherishes his family, his wife
A father that will sacrifice even his life.

A father who knows his salvation God owns,
He watches His glory as he waits to go home.

A father who exemplifies positive display.
We honor and love you. Happy Father's Day!

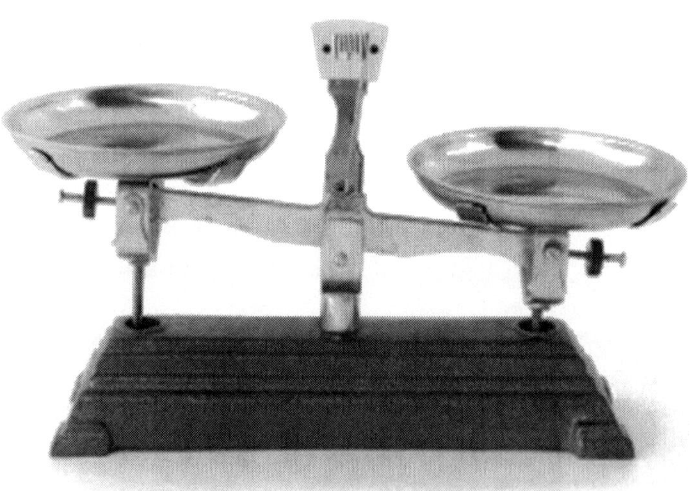

The Natural Order

The passion to teach with splendor and style, the
natural order for rearing a child. The nurture of
parents both male and female promotes the fullness to
balance the scale. When scales are unbalanced, dubiety
breathes. The child loses self where lack is conceived.

When identity's questioned and no answers in sight,
self-esteem falls deeply from shadows of light.
Comfort and nourishment may lack unaware,
search for completeness may leave the soul bare.

The child grows deprived the abundance of life,
searching for love through a husband or wife. As time
passes by, the search empty yet still, then child
having child is another sad pill.

This remedy's temporal for the void still remains. A
hollow-ache and the source of great pain. For the
cycle repeats when the child is unhealed, teaching
those things they found unrevealed.

The well-rounded one finds real love from within. The
seeds planted young for each blossoms a friend. The
mother, the father, their bond forms the cord for
completeness that's balanced through love from the Lord.

REFLECTION
*The one-parent home may produce equal fruit, when an
opposite gender mentors the youth. The natural order,
treasure refined, imparts self-assurance for true peace of mind.*

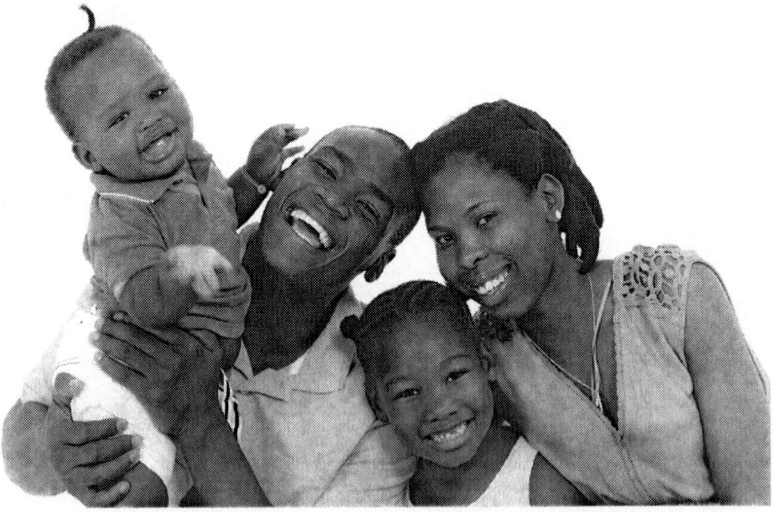

The Ones We Love

Does family mean the world to you, a heart you strive to give?
Does family care enough to share, the life they're meant to live?

Heart to heart and breast to breast. To carry heavy loads.
Ear to hear within the nest. Imparting all you know.

The family is the way we love. Through
faith, the house is run.
The family. Let us care enough to make the family one.

Does family seek a path to find the truth in every plight?
Does family take a stand for peace, to love and not to fight?

A caring hand, a loving eye. The insight to discern.
An open mind, a new insight. Embracing what you learn,

The family is the unity, a bond that's firm and strong.
The family is a melody, a heartbeat in true song.

Let's seek to find the little things that make each one unique.
Let's cherish every attribute that's beautiful to see.

Does family value every work and cherish precious life?
Does family take the time to spend and honor what is right?

The ones we love, let's hold them dear. Take care with what we say.
The ones we love, let's keep them near.
Embrace them every day!

Black Butterfly

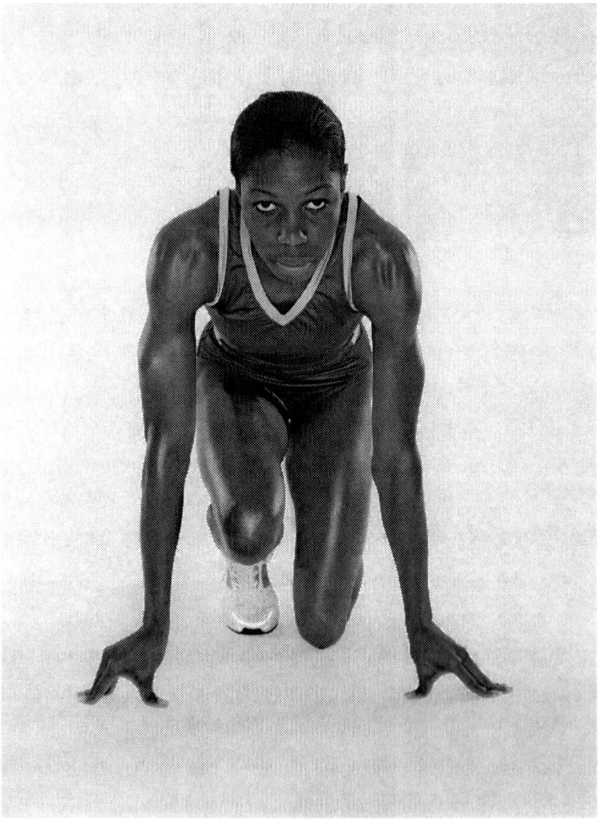

The Power of One

In the shadows of time, one has fought for a cause,
trodden and weary, stumbling while lost.
Searching for such to call all their own,
no dwelling to claim, for they haven't a home.

Stripped of their honor, a deep-seated pain,
robbed of their history through loss of their name.
Oppression still whispers to weaken the mind,
"Surrender resolve and true peace you will find."

Yet there is no peace where there isn't a choice,
The pursuit of free-will is the intellect's voice.
Strength to move forward, grasp sight of the goal,
while justice remains towards the end of the road.

Enlightenment's shared as one travels the path,
while sensing, the fear, the anger, the wrath.
The power of one, so effective a force,
dispelling old mindsets by changing its course.

To mend things undone, one must take a stand.
The power of one; the best part of the plan.
One must be bold. There's a price to be paid,
for the struggle is old; it continues today.

Equality's wrought when one levels the scale,
to fight for a cause where others may fail.
Free-will is a privilege, superior to none,
Let's never discount the true power of one.

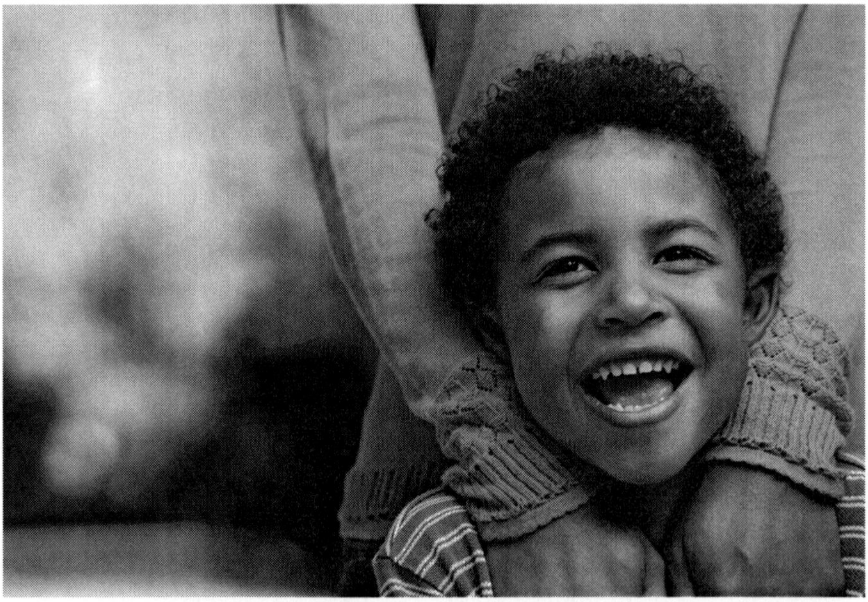

The Voice of a Little Child

Can you hear the rush of the business world
when the sun wakes up the sky?
Can you hear the cries of a little girl when she asks the question, why?
Why must we spend time with her? Why is there excuse?
If the children are our future, what do we have to lose?

Can you hear the voice of a little child when
their questions seem absurd?
Can you hear the voice of a little child when inquisition strikes a nerve?
Why must we be impatient with him? Why must we cut him short?
Let us listen with an open heart and hear a child's report.

Can you hear the roll of the thunder as the white clouds turn to gray?
Can you hear the sobs of a little boy when there's sorrow and dismay?
Why must we be dismissive with him? Why must he be strong?
Is he allowed to shed a tear when all to him is wrong?

Can you hear the voice of a little child when he wants to share his day?
Can you hear the sound of a troubled home when parents are in fray?
Why must we act as if he's not there? Why must he be ignored?
Can we stop and look into his eyes and see what they implore?

If the children are our future, what do we have to lose?
There's mystery in every voice. There's beauty in every youth.
We must strive to have an ear to hear the voice of a precious child.
Come listen with an open mind. Sit down and chat a while.

Black Butterfly

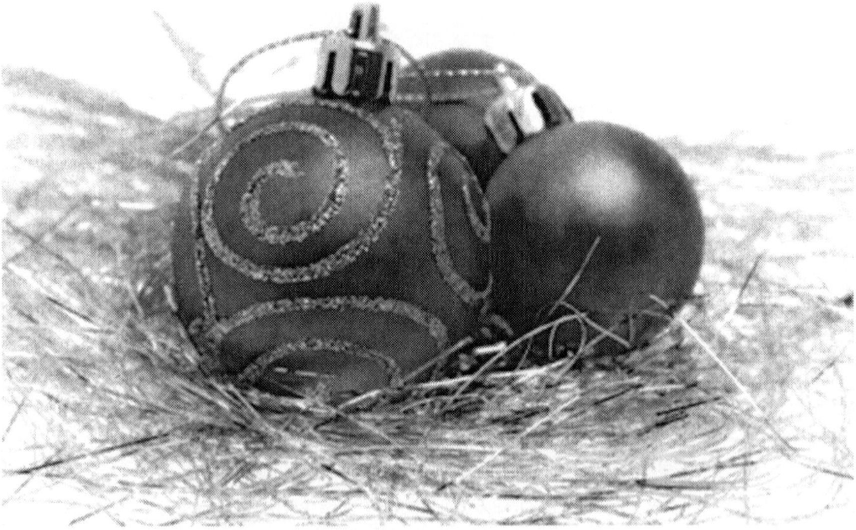

This Christmas

The gift of love, a voice sincere to share with those we hold so dear.
Families gather all around embracing warmth where it is found.

Bosom's swell with love and care as sounds of Christmas fill the air.
Our quality of life refined, a gentle touch, a peace of mind.

Priceless treasure, to express the beauty of His faithfulness.
Sparkling lights, gifts of joy, children playing with their toys.

Tokens of the season's light, yet love's the beauty shining bright.
Spread a little on your path, a special thanks for what we have.

Compassion, tender as a breeze, a gentleness to fill a need.
Let us bask in its display, a splendid light of golden rays.

This Christmas grasp the hope above
and share the precious gift of love.
Merry Christmas

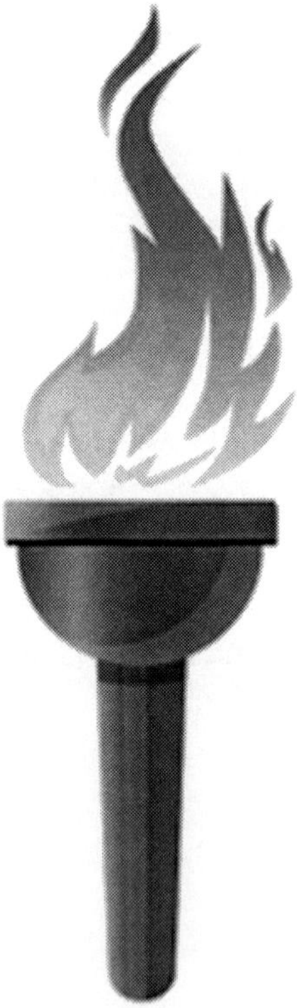

Torch of the Bold

Dedicated to Women of Valor

To strive for the mark of perfection,
one must conceive the stance of the bold.
Pursuit for excellence, the path of direction
to support the endeavors of a common goal.

Your strength and tenacity, a quality inspired.
We support and encourage you in all that you do.
For the end result is a treasure admired;
a commission to unlock the potential of youth.

Striving to develop a team of propriety
requires commitment from your group of support.
Supporting education in a global society,
successful achievement, the greatest report.

Continue to carry the torch of the bold,
enduring the race till the end of the path.
Your triumph, the prize, a rare gift to unfold;
the students of merit, the best of their class.

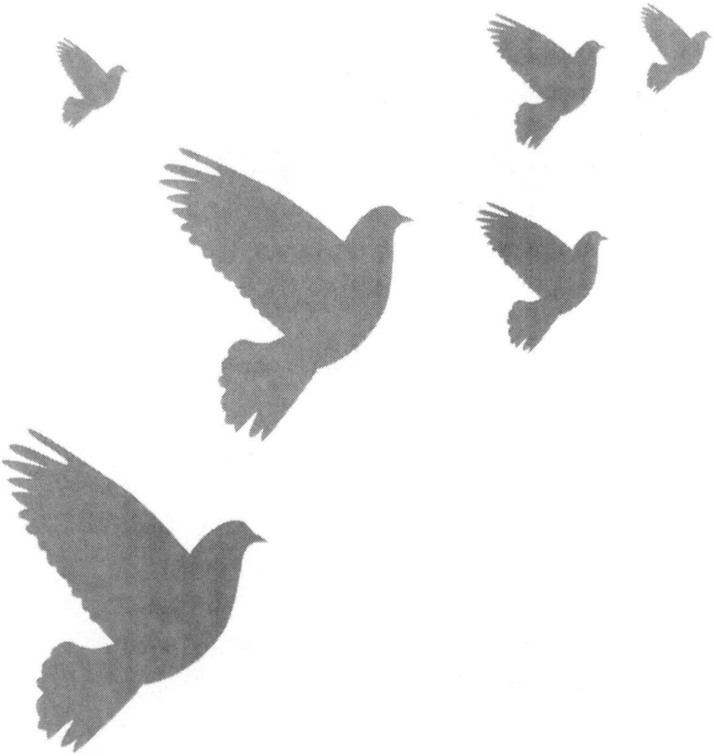

What Do You Believe?

Dear friend, we all are family, unique designs of mystery.
The Father gives each frame a shape, integral, peerless in its place.
Foundation that is sure to stand; body structure strong in plan.

When a friend's encounters ought, heart an ache, in bitter wrought,
an ear to hear when fact's the base, a sounding brass when not the case.
Anointing's nigh unto thy breast, astringency, a sore distress.
What Do You Believe?

One may say they are your friend, through
thick and thin, right to the end,
Yet if one feels they've been transgressed, does wrath endanger holiness?
Communication is the key. Verity, so close to thee.

Yet disdain dwells in bosom lost for rancor's sleep within its walls.
Erstwhile years of friendship wane, shimmers dew in every pane.
A silent tear falls from an eye, as one looks for the reason, why?

Though words seem near, close to your heart,
a voice sincere will never part.
Where lies the tool to prune perception, when mindset's lost in misconception?
To mend the fence within your grasp, adjoin the bridge to fill the gap?
What Do You Believe?

Should we turn and walk away? Is restoration found in fray?
Body formed through every member, bonds arrayed in wondrous splendor.
In retrospect, the Lord of Hosts hath formed the tie that drew us close.

What value's placed on friendship's age? Can we move forward past this stage?
Embracing what we hold so dear, purging thoughts of doubt and fear.
Forgiveness is the central trait to take us from this woeful place.
What Do You Believe?

As we recall past joys and pain, endurance weathered heavy rain.
We need each other in our lives, including those we may not like.
To bask in strength's divinity, embrace silent serenity.

A friendship lost due to dissention is never part of God's intention.
As we take on the life of Christ, each member's perfect in His sight.
His love, the prize for victory to bring the fold to unity.
What Do You Believe?

Why do you love me?

Why do you love me? Why are you kind?
Why are you forgiving? You're loving all the time.
You're so great and so mighty ... awesome and you're wise.
Holy, merciful, sweet and you're mine.
You're forgiving, you are merciful ... you are wise and you are truth.
You are everything and I'm nothing, but you love me. I love you.
Why do you love me? Why are you kind? Why are you forgiving?
You're loving all the time.

Bridge:
God's waiting for me. God's waiting for you.
God's waiting for me. God's waiting for you.
To surrender and repent. Lay it all at His feet.
Surrender and repent. Lay it all at His feet.
He will fill you with His love. Fill you with His peace.
His kindness, goodness, joy ... Is what you need (humility)

God's waiting for me. God's waiting for you.
God's waiting for me. God's waiting for you.
To surrender and repent. Lay it all at His feet.
Surrender and repent. Lay it all at His feet.
He will fill you with His love. Fill you with His peace.
His kindness, goodness, joy ... Is what you need (humility).

Bridge 2
God's waiting for me. God's waiting for you.
God's waiting for me. God's waiting for you.
Trust Him, Have Faith, Obey Him, Always
Trust Him, Have Faith, Obey Him, Always

Fruits of the Spirit
Galatians 5:22-23 But the fruit of the Spirit is love, joy, peace, longsuffering, gentleness, goodness, faith, meekness, temperance: against such there is no law.

Tribute to Maya Angelou

Maya Angelou was born on April 4, 1928 in St. Louis Missouri. She was an accomplished poet, actress and writer. Her journey is one of extraordinary magnitude. She is an inspiration to many that follow her work as well as those they know of her, through signature poetry like, "Phenomenal Woman" and "I Know Why the Cage Bird Sings."

Maya's candid style of writing often inspires recitation in school plays and movies. I remember watching Queen Latifah's, "Beauty Shop," where Alfre Woodard recites, "Phenomenal Woman," as she sways her hips and illustrates the beauty of a woman. I can only imagine the number of women that have imitated the same recitation. With certainty, Maya's work has touched many of us. Her legacy left an impact that sears me to the core and certainly inspires this tribute.

Maya Angelou was a profound artist; she was a magnificent fashion of beauty and grace, paving the way for African-American women in many areas. Maya Angelou was the first African-American woman to write the screen play, "Georgia." This screen play was also nominated for a Pulitzer Prize. Her timeline of accomplishments include a school of music and dance, a role in Alex Haley's, "Roots," and much more.

Truly, my heart was saddened when I learned of her passing on May 28, 2014. I'm sure many can attest to the awesome gift her life and work left on this earth. Can't you hear her poetry even now? I hear her poetry in every challenge. I hear her poetry in every struggle. I hear her poetry in every accomplishment and undoubtedly, every victory.

In Maya's last tweet, she said, "Listen to yourself and in that quietude, you might hear the voice of God." I will forever honor and cherish the memory of Maya Angelou. Her work is my mentor. Her voice guides my writing; her legacy, my strength; her passion, my peace. Thank you, Maya Angelou.

Timeline of Maya Angelou

1954 through 1955 – Angelou toured Europe with a production of the opera.

1957 – Recorded her first album, "Calypso Lady."

1958 – Angelou moved to New York, where she joined the Harlem Writers Guild. She acted in Jean Genet's Off-Broadway production, "The Blacks," and performed "Cabaret for Freedom."

1960 – Angelo moved to Cairo, Egypt where she served as editor of the English language weekly *The Arab Observer.*

1961 – She moved to Ghana, where she taught at the University of Ghana's School of Music and Drama. She worked as a feature editor for *The African Review* and wrote for *The Ghanaian Times.*

1964 – Returned to America to help Malcolm X build his new organization of African American Unity.

1970 – Published "I Know Why the Caged Bird Sings," also received the Chubb Fellowship from Yale University. Angelou has received over 50 honorary degrees.

1972 – Film "Georgia, Georgia" came out. Angelou wrote the screenplay and composed the score. Her script was the first ever written by an African American woman to be filmed, and was nominated for a Pulitzer Prize.

1977 – Appeared in the television adaptation of Alex Haley's "Roots."

1982 – Joined the faculty at Wake Forest University as a Professor of American Studies.

1993 – Appeared in John Singleton's Poetic Justice. Won Grammy Award for Best Spoken Word Or Non-Musical Album for "On the Pulse of Morning."

1995 – Won Grammy Award for Best Spoken Word On Non-Musical Album for "Phenomenal Woman."

1996 – Directed her first feature film, "Down in the Delta."

2000 – Awarded the Presidential Medal of Arts.

2002 – Won Grammy Award for Best Spoken Word Album with "A Song Flung Up To Heaven."

2008 – Composed poetry for and narrated the award-winning documentary The Black Candle, directed by M.K. Asante. Also awarded the Lincoln Medal.

2011 – Received the Presidential Medal of Freedom from President Barack Obama at the White House.

May 23, 2014 – Angelou sent her last tweet: "Listen to yourself and in that quietude you might hear the voice of God."

May 28, 2014 – Maya Angelou passes away in her Winston Salem home. She made her transition to be with Father God on May 28, 2014.

About the Author

Lorna Jackie Wilson was born in 1964 in Detroit, Michigan to Carrie Jean Wilson. At the age of four, she was placed in foster care. This placement stemmed from a number of reasons. Reflections of her childhood with her mother and siblings draw memories where fish nets hung from the ceiling with Polaroid photos hanging in the balance as the record player's needle dropped to spin songs like, "Me and Mrs. Jones" and "Lost in a Masquerade."

Most of her childhood memories are fond as she eagerly anticipated each day playing with her siblings outside. In those days, Lorna and her siblings were rarely in the home because her mother's rule was that you stayed outside until dinner was called. After dinner, you went back outside until the street lights came on. Little did she know that her mother had an addiction to drugs.

Therefore, when foster care came to take her and her siblings away, she was distraught and torn. Yet at the age of 10, she was returned to her mother and she and her siblings reunited only to be separated again at the age of 13. Lorna was in and out of foster care for 11 years of her life. While the journey reveals a combination of pain and loss, it also reveals love, laughter and accomplishment.

The last foster home Lorna entered was while pregnant with her first child. Acie Levingston Spraddling is the foster mother that introduced her to Jesus Christ. Acie led by example. Her lifestyle of Christian living led Lorna to follow Acie around like a little lost puppy, hungry and thirsty to know God the way she knew Him. This is where singing and writing first began.

At the age of 18, Lorna made a decision to pursue higher education, she enrolled in Detroit Business Institute (DBI) and earned a Word Processing

Specialist Diploma. At that time, DBI had a job placement program which led to her employment with Detroit Public Schools (DPS).

At the age of 25, Lorna took a leave of absence from DPS and joined the United States Army. She graduated top of her class as the Distinguished Honor Graduate. She was offered a position by the general of the battalion. However, since she was on leave of absence from DPS, she returned to her job.

From 1985 to 2006, Lorna retained employment with DPS. The educational experience motivated her to pursue a degree. In 2005, Lorna earned her bachelor's degree from Davenport University. In 2006, she began employment with Oak Park Schools. In 2007, she went on to earn a Master's degree in Business Education from Ashford University.

In 2009, Lorna joined Detroit World Outreach. This is her church home where an awesome worship experience takes place every day under the leadership of Bishop Ben and Dr. Charisse Gibert.

In 2012, Lorna earned a 2nd Masters from Kaplan University in Information Technology.

Lorna is also the mother of four beautiful children, Wanavia, Celeste, Matthew and Christian; all of which support her singing, writing, and computer training school. She couldn't have done it without them.

In 2013, she earned a trophy as one of the runner ups in a National Singing Contest sponsored by William Beaumont Hospital in Royal Oak, Michigan. In the same year, she also started her own business, i.e., The Next Level Computer Training School. Lorna is passionate about computer literacy and provides training with a level of enthusiasm that her students love.

References

American Journal-Constitution (2010). Timeline: Maya Angelou's Life, retrieved from
http://www.ajc.com, June 1, 2014

King James Bible (2014). retrieved from
http://www.kingjamesbibleonline.org/

Royalty Free Images (2014). retrieved from
www.gettyimages.com

World Trade Center Bombing (2014). retrieved from
http://en.wikipedia.org/wiki/Collapse of the World Trade Center
Original uploader was Pauljoffe at en.wikipedia

CPSIA information can be obtained at www.ICGtesting.com
Printed in the USA
LVOW12s2250090814

398251LV00003B/184/P